To be honest, this is the first book I have read that focuses on PTSD. What was interesting to me was that there are many factors that cause PTSD. What was more interesting was the fact that there are many pathways one can follow that will allow one to move away from PTSD. The book now has me thinking about my situation and what my pathway might be.
A very refreshing read."

—*Kent Hillhouse, Major General (ret)U.S. Army*

"It should be mandatory reading for every elected public official about what war and conflict can do to those who serve, along with their families and community. The title of this book tells that what many veterans, men and women, have done for their country—much of the battle is fought in the minds of veterans when they return home to walk in peace."

—*Joe Cotchett, retired Colonel US Army Special Forces (Airborne) Officer and Judge Advocate General's Corps*

"This book needs to get out to the masses that are still in denial, frustrated, and Angry. They simply need to let go, and your book will lead them gently down that path."

—*Charles Collier, Combat Medic 101st Airborne; '68/'69 Vietnam*

"Occasionally traumatic, but always touching, these heartfelt and cathartic short stories and poems will send the reader careening into an array of emotions while bringing a deep understanding of the burden of trauma that anyone can suffer."

—*Donna Colson, Mayor, Burlingame, California*

"This anthology allows our Veterans to tell their stories on their own terms. They are raw and personal, and at times, shocking and painful. They are also healing and need to be heard. As I read them, I grow even closer to my cherished Veteran patients".

—*James Chang MD, Hand Surgeon, VA Palo Alto Health Care System Professor & Chief of Plastic Surgery, Stanford University*

"Permission to Walk in Peace is a remarkable anthology of poems, stories, and essays by military veterans. The contributors deliver searing examinations of the traumas from their combat experiences and profoundly intimate and unflinching accounts of their journey towards healing, repair, and reconciliation. Reading and rereading these accounts is an inspiration, illuminating how lives can be made whole again—with beauty, strength, and purpose."

—*Robert S. Pesich, author of "Model Organism," editor and publisher, Swan Scythe Press*

"You are my strength who carries me today with angels showing me the way. You are my life song, who touches my soul. You break through the darkness, revealing your glorious light. You are the I AM, the ONE whose glory shines through to show these Veterans the way. Amen!"

—*Carmen Montano, Mayor, Milpitas, California*

Permission to Walk in Peace

Permission to Walk in Peace

Stories of Healing from Trauma as Told by Combat Veterans

Edited by G. Craige Edgerton

Alive Book Publishing

Permission to Walk in Peace
Stories of Healing from Trauma as Told by Combat Veterans
Copyright © 2025 by G. Craig Edgerton, Editor

All rights reserved.
No part of this book may be reproduced or transmitted in any form or by any means without written permission from the publisher and editor.

Additional copies may be ordered from the publisher for educational, business, promotional or premium use. For information, contact ALIVE Book Publishing at: alivebookpublishing.com.

Book Design by Alex Johnson

ISBN 13
978-1-63132-255-6

Library of Congress Control Number: 2025906666

Library of Congress Cataloging-in-Publication Data is available upon request.

First Edition

Published in the United States of America by
ALIVE Book Publishing
an imprint of Advanced Publishing LLC
3200 A Danville Blvd., Suite 204, Alamo, California 94507
alivebookpublishing.com

PRINTED IN THE UNITED STATES OF AMERICA

10 9 8 7 6 5 4 3 2 1

This book is dedicated to all the counselors at all the Vet Centers nationwide who have tirelessly assisted veterans who have returned from war or experienced other military trauma in finding their path toward peace.

Their dedication is truly remarkable!

Specifically, this book is dedicated to Daniel Boitano from the San Jose, California Vet Center, who has counseled most of the veterans who contributed to it. His considerable concern for his veterans is remarkable and to be commended.

CONTENTS

DEDICATION	VII
FOREWORD	XIII
INDEX OF AUTHOR WRITINGS	XIV
INTRODUCTION	15
CHAPTER 1 — EXPERIENCE	19
Mortar Raid	21
Sargent Selbie's War	25
It Wasn't All Bad	27
Clearing The Field	33
Ambush Patrol October 1968	31
Fire in the Sky	33
The Letter	35
Hearts and Minds	39
Lost and Real	41
Faces	43
Remembering Sandwich lady	45
Sunny Day, Baghdad	47
Lost Leg, I	49
Lost Leg, II	51
From the Back of the Truck How I Remember Vietnam, I	53
From the Back of the Truck How I Remember Vietnam, II	55
From the Back of the Truck How I Remember Vietnam, III	57
From the Back of the Truck How I Remember Vietnam, IV	59
Nothing Special	63
Smells of Neville	71
Denied	73
You Decide	75
Depression and Suicide	79
Ode to the Unknown Warrior	81

Hostile Fire Pay	83
Almost	89
Making Monsters	81
Staying Alive	93
First Blood October 1968	101
CHAPTER II — HANDRAILS	103
Recovery	105
Depression	107
I Was Her Son	109
The Door	111
The Mirage	113
Hero's Journey	115
Captain Casey	119
Veteran's Day Parade	121
Farewell	123
Why Vietnam?	125
We Went	127
Falling Apart	129
Memorial	131
Fri 24 November 19	133
Getting to Sleep	135
Kids at Play	137
Huckeropter	139
Reparations	141
Coming Home	143
War Sucks	147
War Supporters	149
War Protesters	151
pOETRY	153
Sacrifice	155
Quiet Patriotism	157
The Plan	159

PTSD	161
Helping a Brother Out	163
The Little Box	165
Homeless Bum	169
CHAPTER III—MENDING FENCES	171
Mending Fences	173
Tapestry	175
Energies	193
Thank You For Your Service	195
Healing From Disappointment	199
Disappointment	201
Home Again	203
My Country	205
Where Your Dreams Began	207
Abandoned No More	209
Liberation	213
Reparations	215
Welcome Home	217
Lost on the Path No More	219
A Knotty Situation	221
A Thread I follow	229
Don't Say Goodbye to Nobody	231
I Am Home	233
Haiku Vietnam	239
Surly You Know Private Nelson	241
Paying It Forward	243
The Light of Fire	245
The Magical Room	247
I AM. I WAS	249
An Internal War	251
Dumpster Diving	255
Remnants of a Past Life	257

Yellow Palace	259
Military Veteran's Dog tags	261
Kintsugi Haikus	265
Judgment	267
His Name is on the Wall	269
It Happened Unexpectedly	271
Common Ground	273
Potato Duty	275
Mr. L	277
Service	281
Korean War Veterans Speech	283
Moon Landing	287
Crumbled, Humbled, and Welcomed Home	289
Redemption	291
Crows	295
CHAPTER IV — FRIENDS AND FAMILY	297
Letter from a Veteran's Brother	297
Letters Home, Second Platoon ECHO	303
Abilene Airport	307
Helicopter OH-6A 67-16162	309
BIOGRAPHIES	311

For further inforamtion about
"Permission to Walk in Peace,"
its contributing authors
and
Veteran's Support Organizations
visit
VeteransCourage.org
or scan this code

FOREWORD

The title of this book tells us that what many veterans, men and women, have done for our country - much of the battle is fought in the minds of veterans when they return home to walk in peace.

It should be mandatory reading for every elected public official about what conflict and war can do to those who serve, along with their families and community. The Chapters demonstrate the trauma that so many went through and the useless power displays of people who never wore a uniform. The individual stories all tell a different narrative, but with all having the same basic theme — that conflicts only destroy innocent people and veterans never find complete peace when they are finished serving.

War all comes down to political power, whether it be Korea, Vietnam, Afghanistan or current conflicts around the world - by those who want to send people like veterans in this book to do their pointless power grab. It tells a tragic but true story of what combat veterans experience in all our wars.

—*Joe Cotchett, Colonel, US Army (Ret.) Special Forces (Airborne)*
Judge Advocate General's Corps, Legion of Merit

INDEX OF AUTHOR WRITINGS

Bill Noyes   25, 31, 35, 45, 63, 75, 93, 101, 161, 265

G. Craige Edgerton   27, 49, 51, 71, 81, 105, 115, 121, 127, 143, 157,
                      165, 175, 195, 207, 217, 221, 247, 249, 251,
                      255, 259, 269, 271, 277, 291, 297, 307

Doug Nelson   53, 55, 57, 59, 119, 139, 205, 241

Jaime Johnson   29, 33, 43, 47, 73, 89, 109, 137, 163, 203, 243,
                      257, 267, 281

Jim Marney-Petix   21, 39, 79, 91, 105, 107, 125, 133, 135, 149,
                      151, 228

Marshall Burgamy   83, 295

Nick Butterfield   41, 131, 141, 147, 153, 231, 239, 287

Sunny Dosanjh   111, 113, 123, 129, 169, 173, 193, 199, 201,
                      209, 213, 219, 233, 245, 261, 273, 275, 283,
                      289

INTRODUCTION

Permission to Walk in Peace began with a group of military veterans in a room sharing their experiences of combat. Over weeks and months, it evolved into discovering common traits they all had on their road to recovery. They decided that road was important enough to be shared with not only other veterans but anyone dealing with trauma or PTSD.

Trauma is trauma. The details vary, but a common thread of healing exists when one permits oneself to walk that road toward peace. Whether it be combat, divorce, sexual trauma, childhood trauma, a serious illness or disease, or any other trauma, recovery to a normal, productive life is not only possible but happens often. Rarely is it done alone, and it almost always requires some counseling and a support network. The veteran writers of *Permission to Walk in Peace* walked that journey toward home and decided to share it with others.

The veteran writers who contributed to this book have chosen to find a positive outcome from their trauma and share some of their journey. It is not a manual that provides psychological counseling but an insight into how a group of veterans have coped. Anyone with trauma or PTSD is encouraged to seek qualified counseling.

One of the book's themes is **Weaving a Tapestry**, which consists of tapestries of fabrics with many hues and colors woven together with gold, silver, and other precious threads. The fabrics represent the encounters each has experienced in life, resulting in unique, one-of-a-kind pieces of artwork: a rebuilt and renewed life.

The other theme is **Kintsugi**, the Japanese art of reassembling broken pottery with a precious lacquer mixture. It is a perfect analogy for anyone experiencing trauma. These veterans' lives were shattered, and they are reassembling those lives through their writings.

The writings are helpful in and of themselves, but the greater good is sharing them with others.

The writing styles reflect that artistic endeavor with poems, essays, and stories. They have attempted to portray their stories artistically but keep them factual. That artistic element is designed to reach a deeper inner connection with the reader instead of just telling the facts.

The veterans are from different wars and times, mainly Vietnam. They want to share how they have dealt with their trauma so that other veterans, family members, or anyone who has experienced trauma can glimpse into their process. Their experiences are theirs, and each person's experience with trauma will be unique to her or him. A shift in thinking is possible, and it is hoped their stories are a catalyst for that shift.

The book does not follow a traditional format because there is no single storyline. It is a woven tapestry composed of poems, stories, and essays each writer has written to deal with their trauma. It is their practice of Kintsugi, reassembling the broken pieces of their lives into a new work of art. The book is divided into three main sections: Experience, Handrails, and Mending Fences. A short addendum of family and friends is added at the end.

Experience is the story of what happened. Combat trauma usually results in PTSD and is a different kind of trauma. It is no more or less impactful than other traumas, but it is unique in its conditions. Some of the stories are graphic and may be hard to read. Many deal with the impact on the innocent locals. But all are firsthand accounts by those who were there.

Handrails is how the writers dealt with or are dealing with their traumas after leaving the military. Avoidance, too much booze or drugs, inability to keep a job, divorce, and anger are just some of the common responses in their return to civilian life. These are the years before they decided to face their demons head-on and get help. The word Handrails comes from using them on ships in the Navy to climb stairs. Ship stairs are notoriously steep and, without handrails, almost impossible to climb. These stories tell of the handrails the veterans used to manage their lives despite their trauma.

Mending Fences also came from one of the veterans in a poignant story of reconnection with his father. It became an analogy for mending the broken psyches the veterans were and are still facing. This is the most important section of the book as it expresses the positive outcomes of facing their trauma head-on and coming to peace. They have all decided to grow from their experience instead of being a victim of it. That is the time they have given themselves *Permission to Walk in Peace*.

A note to the reader: Do not read this book like a novel with a consistent storyline leading to a conclusion. Each section and story within that section stands alone. It helps to remember that this is a tapestry of stories with no beginning or end. One can interact with the tapestry from many angles. The stories also represent the broken pieces of their lives and the reassembling of them, Kintsugi. The writers hope the reader is inspired to create their own tapestry of healing, whether for themselves or a loved one, and use Kintsugi as a model to reconstruct their lives.

If so, this book has been a success.

CHAPTER 1
Experience

*"I hate war as only a Soldier who has lived it can,
only as one who has seen its brutality, its futility, its stupidity."*
—Dwight Eisenhower

Trauma is trauma, be it the unexpected death of a loved one, sexual misconduct, combat, childhood abuse, an automobile accident, or anything that fits the definition—**an experience that produces psychological injury or pain.** Trauma is not limited to military veterans. People experience trauma in many different ways. This first chapter, Experience, consists of writings about the time these veterans experienced their trauma. Some of the stories are graphic and may be hard to read, but they are necessary to understand their experience.

Studies have shown that combat trauma sufferers tend to have PTSD longer and more intensely than those with civilian trauma. Men reporting combat as their worst trauma were more likely to have lifetime PTSD, delayed PTSD symptom onset, and unresolved PTSD symptoms, and to be unemployed, fired, divorced, and physically abusive to their spouses than men reporting other traumas as their worst experience.

These veterans believe that they have a choice on how to deal with their trauma. They can be victims, or they can choose to grow from their experience. These veterans have chosen the latter.

Veterans who have chosen to deal with and grow from their trauma are in a unique position to share their stories. This project began as a way for military veterans with PTSD or trauma to write about their experiences of recovery and share those insights with their friends and family. They wanted to answer the question: "How have we overcome our trauma, and can we share the lessons we have learned with others?" As the project developed, it became clear that **the lessons learned applied to anyone with trauma, whether military or civilian.** These writers intend this book to be for everyone who has dealt with trauma.

Mortar Raid
Jim Marney-Petix

Tink, tink, tink, sluuuuuup, thoomb! I was sound asleep a second ago, but there's no mistaking that sound.

Tink, tink, tink, sluuuuuup, thoomb! One hand wraps around the hard plastic of my rifle, the other snags my web gear. "In coming!"

Tink, tink, tink, sluuuuuup, thoomb! Shove my feet into my boots and out the door!

Tink, tink, tink, sluuuuuup, thoomb! Hang time is about 10 seconds, a good crew can get ten in the air before the first one hits.

Tink, tink, tink, sluuuuuup, thoomb! We don't dare use a light and make ourselves targets.

Tink, tink, tink, sluuuuuup, thoomb! Fortunately, there's a little moon shining through the cloud cover, and I can make out the bunker as a blacker black against a black sky.

Tink, tink, tink, sluuuuuup, thoomb! The first round lands. It's not close, but the flash from the explosion destroys my night vision. Blind, I run face-first into the back of the bunker. "Shit! Shit! Shit!" I have blood in my mouth and I'm sure my nose is broken. The second round lands. I feel along the rough weave of the sandbags until I find the opening and pile in.

I'm curled up on the floor in a back corner with my fingers in my ears and my mouth open, trying to equalize the pressure so the sound doesn't burst my eardrums. It fills my universe. It pounds me like a mallet. I hear screaming. It might be me, I can't tell.

As abruptly as it started, it's over. My ears are ringing, and I'm dizzy as hell. I'm grateful to be alive, but I've got a job to do. Shaking my head to clear it, I scoot over to the door and take up a position, looking back into the camp. Sometimes, our little playmates like to blow through the razor wire while the rounds are falling and send in sappers with bags of explosives to throw in the bunkers. Bunkers are great for keeping explosions out, but they're even better for keeping explosions in. It would only take a chunk of C4 about the size of a grapefruit to turn us into a thousand pounds of tomato paste. So, blinded by the flashes and deafened by the explosions, it's my job to kill anything that doesn't look or sound American.

After an hour, it's clear there won't be a sapper attack, so the squad leader starts handing out cans of food. What do I get? Ham and lima beans. Hell, even the starving locals won't eat ham and limas! The ham tastes like slimy pencil erasers, and the limas are the consistency of hominy grits mixed with lard. Kelly's set up a stove, but I don't bother. Heating won't make it taste any better. Instead, I hand him my canteen cup. What I get back is 20 ounces of hot coffee—two packets of government-issued instant, tainted with iodine from the water purification tablets. God! that tastes good!

My nose dripped enough blood on my t-shirt that it's sticking to my chest, but the bleeding itself seems to have stopped. To check, I use a little of the coffee to wash the blood off my face and dry off on my sleeves. My nose doesn't seem to be broken, and I'm not bleeding, I guess I won't be getting a Purple Heart after all, but my shirt's wet, and I'm starting to shiver.

Fortunately, I was wrapped up in my poncho liner when the shooting started, and I brought it with me. Best piece of equipment the Army ever made. This nylon quilt is big enough to be a blanket, weighs nothing, is warm, dries in ten minutes, and is silky smooth against the skin. If the damned thing would just learn to cook, I'd marry it. I wrap it around me, wet shirt and all, and feel the warmth seeping back into my body.

I really get into the night. Off to my right, I hear a generator running at the other end of the compound. Behind me, a couple of guys are talking about their families in whispers. Off to my left-front about 50 yards away, I hear someone walking around outside the next bunker. To my left rear in the village a quarter mile away, I hear a baby crying. Not being able to see just powers up my hearing.

My nose is cleared up and working again. I wish it weren't. Every guy in the bunker has been out on a piss break at least twice. The spot they use is only ten feet away. It's starting to smell like a urinal around here.

The cloud cover cleared off before sunrise. Because there are no clouds to light up and turn pink, the sunrise is completely uneventful. The world goes from dark to light, and the sun's up. Bleaa.

The countryside is beautiful: jungle-covered mountains to the west, Pacific to the east, every inch of land between terraced for rice cultivation. It's almost an Iron-Age lifestyle out here: water buffalo for draft animals; hand tools to get the work done; light, cooking, and heat from wood fires; communication by walking over to someone and actually talking to them. Then I look at the "civilization" we've brought: razor wire, sandbags, ugly green buildings, generators that run all night, noise pollution, light pollution, air pollution. Is it really an improvement?

We get the word to stand down and start walking to the mess hall. The first chore of the day is latrine detail. The guys stuck with this job drag out the cut-down 55-gallon drums that sit under the holes in the latrines, pour fuel oil in them, and set them on fire. So, like every other morning, we eat breakfast surrounded by the smell of burning shit.

Forty-three more days, and I'm outta here.

Sergeant Selbie's War
March or April 1968
Bill Noyes

We met Sergeant Selbie when we transferred from Basic at Ft. Lewis, WA, to AIT at Ft. Polk, LA. He became our platoon training sergeant and marched us, in his turn, to and from training stations during the two months we learned infantry tactics at "Tigerland".

Sgt. Selbie was notable for several things. He was a quiet and mild-tempered guy, with a strangely creased pug nose. He marched us and harassed us, much as all the others had or would do because that was his job. But Selbie had our confidence and instant attention because he could tell us his war stories. He was the only trainer we had had who had actually fought in combat during the war.

All the others, including most of the demonstrators and instructors in our training, if they had even been to the war zone at all, had served in non-combat units, usually outside the infantry. They were not always forthcoming about this information, but we learned to pry. We could increasingly see that we were destined for the infantry war, so we hungered for the experience that might help our chances.

Selbie was the only one who could or would share his honest experience at war. He gave us his humble accounting of the medal he'd won when he spotted the glint of a sniper's scope, pushed aside his lieutenant, and was shot across the nose. He had other stories about life in the field and what we could expect when we got there.

We respected Sgt. Selbie for his honest assessment of our chances at war. The quiet time in the barracks always promised a meaningful retelling of his stories in our preparation for the fight. Our days turned to weeks, then became a month when Sgt. Selbie was marching us back from a shooting range. Four abreast one dark evening along a roadside put Selbie out in the road. A deuce and a half ran him down and killed him. We still had a month to go in our training.

It Wasn't All Bad
G. Craige Edgerton

It wasn't all bad.
There was the dangling leg,
Wrapped by the corpsman,
Desperately trying to save it…
And him.
As the chopper whisked him away.

But it wasn't all bad.

Flashes from the thick jungle
Snipers harassing with ancient weapons.
Bullets missed.
105 howitzers silence them.

But it wasn't all bad.

Sweating out the ambush
While on patrol.
Trip wire?
Just a branch…this time.

But it wasn't all bad.

The quiet before dusk
Watching the sun sink
Into Laos, the song of jungle calls.
Calm before the long, dark night.

Really, it wasn't all bad.

Clearing The Field
Jaime Lee Johnson

The night is dark, stars above.
The radio crackles with mindless traffic.
I listen for the call. Again, nothing.
My gaze returns to the night sky.
I wonder what stars point home, then …
I hear a familiar voice over the radio.
He calls for help and I spring into action.

We're on the road, speeding. Speeding.
They're so far away.
The HMMWV is quiet, minds racing.
We're too slow.

On a bridge now, dismounted.
Peering into the dark.
The sergeant next to me orders a star cluster.
With a thump, we light up the sky.
We all aim into the illuminated area, searching, ready.
Only the shadows move.

Back into the HMMWV, but not to return.
We move to the field, and wait.
A soldier next to me jumps out. I grab him.
"It's pitch black, Auggie!" I yell and pull him
back into the vehicle.

Dismounted again, now in the field.
NODs mounted, eyes awash with the green glow.
In formation, slow, steady, searching, waiting.

Soldiers to my left, shanties to my right.
Shadows and darkness all around.
I step over a log and into the IR shadow.
It's deeper that I thought, then SNAP!
"Shit!", I mutter. I wince at my own sound.
My eyes close, as I await the round that sends me home.
And wait. It never comes.

Back into the HMMWV and on the road.
Adrenaline still rushing.
My thoughts rage as we disappear into the night.

Ambush Patrol. October, 1968
Bill Noyes

My heart is black. It's my turn to lead the way. My black heart helps me melt easily into the night. No moon, nor stars, will light my way. My body and my mind follow my thumping heart. They are like ghosts called to a séance. Their quiet whispers beg caution. They screech fear but without dread.

It's mine to step forward to lead the patrol to our ambush position hidden amongst the trees. Our squad will lead an ARVN squad, to show them how it's done. Too many of them and it is my first patrol. Still, they must learn since it is their war.

Choices are complicated in war but water fills the paddies, so the dike seems the only way to go. My foot feels the unseen path. Their following sucking steps slide through the mud behind me as my ears reach past their noises. I step carefully forward.

My last step sinks quickly into bottomless liquid. I am submerged into the liquid darkness as I grip my rifle like a useless toy. Thrashing, the man behind me pulls me up and out. Obvious teamwork saves the night, if not my pride.

Quiet returns but our patrol has ended. The leader decided to set up there, strung along the dike, and forgo the wood line. I had already shown the ARVN the important lesson about how to find the farmer's well.

Fire in the Sky
Jaime Lee Johnson

Sound asleep and dreaming of someplace other than the city of heat and danger. A familiar sound of running on rocks wakes me from my peaceful slumber. But this time, it sounds more frantic as I hear many pairs of boots speeding past in different directions.

I rise from my soft bed and open the door to my room to see what the commotion is all about. Before me is a blizzard of chaos filled with soldiers frantically putting on gear as they rush to the motorpool. HMMWVs, 1113s, Bradleys, Abrams, and other manner of mechanized destruction spinning to life with a thunderous roar that fills the hot night air. The stench of diesel almost chokes me as I step out into the fray of foot traffic and ask what's going on. A grizzled soldier with an M4 says, "Look up!"

I do as he says and what I see is almost beyond comprehension. What I saw some may describe as shooting stars. If only it were true. For the night sky wasn't filled with shooting stars, but with tracer fire and in every direction. I couldn't tell what was tracer and what was a star, there was so much of it.

I don't know how long I stood there, but it was long enough for me to feel a need to breathe. For I had been holding my breath since I saw what seemed like a living nightmare.

A moment passes and just as I gain some semblance of self awareness, a HMMWV comes speeding down a road leading to the panic filled motorpool. A large man jumps out, wearing PT clothing, DCU boots, and an unsecured helmet. He's screaming and it takes me a moment to understand him. A lull in the noise allowed what he was trying to tell everyone become clear. "Stand down! Stand down! Iraq just beat Kuwait in a soccer game!"

The Letter
Bill Noyes of B2/22nd, 1969

The actual letter was inscribed on March 5, 1968, as translated after I brought it home. It was this letter that I'd picked up from the battlefield near the Ben Cui plantation in 1969. It was the discarded remnant of a life that had belonged to my enemy. It had been read and discarded as useless information in this war by an intelligence operative. I'd picked it from the ground as a curious scrap of secret history rather than let it evaporate as it would in time, as would its owner, the corpse lying at my feet.

He had died in the small battle the night before and had been searched that morning while I had been gone on maneuvers. From his near nakedness his few irrelevant possessions left scattered on the ground, he seemed an especially pathetic consequence of war. I could not guess what secret the foreign scripted letter might hold, but I was curious. He had carried it a long way and kept it especially close to him in battle. I took one last picture of him and his letter. No golden treasure would be my reward for my victorious combat, merely my curiosity satisfied.

Home again seven months later, I put an ad on a college board to find a translator for the letter. I'd kept it for many months and barely made it home alive. I supposed it would have been merely discarded, unread, along with all my unnecessary junk had I not made it home alive. A Vietnamese student agreed to do the job for a small sum and in a week I finally knew what my battle treasure actually said. I merely trusted his accuracy then, and trust sufficiently its meaning now.

My dearest love,
I received another letter from you the day before yesterday, March 3. In your letter you said that you haven't received any mail from me even the

one I sent on Feb 17th. Therefore, I have to write this letter immediately otherwise you will wait so long.

My love, so you are going out to the battlefield, aren't you? Last Sunday, when coming back home, Miss Tuyet told me that you were about to go on an operation pretty soon; but in your previous letter, you still didn't tell me anything about it.

If you have to leave, I would like you not to worry about anything, even about me. You should think of nothing else but your duty, and try to achieve victory so that the day when you return, we can be happy together. We are now so far away from each other, and I don't know when we can see each other again.

As for me, everything is going as usual. I haven't had any day off since Tet (New Year Festival), and it was not until last Sunday that I was allowed to come home for a visit. But as soon as I got home, I had a really bad time with my Mother. She blamed and scorned me the minute she saw me on the porch. Someone had said that your parents already made the proposal of our marriage and something else I don't know, but Mom got upset.

My dearest love, whenever I came home and was scorned like that, I always thought about it for days and was very sad. As to you, I understand you more and more, and love you very much but I don't know whether we will be able to see each other again or not. For the present time, my love, please forget everything I have just said. We will wait until the day of victory, when you come back, then we will talk about it.

My dearest love, last Sunday when I visited your parents, they gave me your diary which you had asked them to. Your Father also told me that you were sick and looked very thin when he went up to visit you the other day. I am so sad and worry very much to hear that you still have to go out fighting the battle while you are sick like that. I know that you are now at a place which is very, very far from here but I cannot imagine where it is. My love, please take good care of yourself and recover soon so that you won't be behind your friends in your duty. As for me, I was sick also the other day and had to stay in bed for two days, but now I am already fine.

My dearest love, please don't think about what I have said and don't be sad. You wrote in your diary that you are afraid that I will be sad when *reading the diary. I must confess that I was a little bit sad at first; but it was all my fault. I couldn't have a chance to talk with you more so that you can understand me.*

Now that I have known you more, I promise that I won't be sad, and my love, promise me that you won't think about it anymore either.

I have to stop here. May God bring you good health and happiness.

Your love,

"I hope to see you as soon as possible."

Over the years, because of poor storage, the ink has blurred and migrated throughout the letter's page. Even parts of the type-written translation have become chipped away or stained. Clearly, such human residue is not meant to outlast the eons. Troubled times should belong to the tormentors and not burden future victims as unwanted ghosts. The living always have more to occupy their attention, it seems, than they are actually prepared to handle.

The nameless enemy who had brought his cherished letter all the way from the north over months of travel to the Saigon vicinity has long ago molded and washed away; pelted by countless monsoons. His cherished letter, carried with him like no other possession into a stripped-down battle, might have sustained his spirits, then. But it is useful no more. Still, it is an interesting remnant and a story to be told.

Hearts and Minds
Jim Marney-Petix

We were patrolling through a rural village. In this area, every hut had a bunker in front of it. The bunker was a wooden room with a narrow doorway at one end, a bench running down each side for sitting on, and all of it buried under three feet of dirt. When a firefight started, or the artillery came in, everyone in the hut would run out to the bunker to wait it out. A middle-aged woman would sit in the doorway with a toddler in her lap. When she saw us coming, she would hold up the child and yell, "Okay baby san! Okay baby san!" over and over in the sometimes vain hope that we wouldn't immediately start shooting or throwing in frags. The bunker was built when the hut was built, so the dirt has had plenty of time to compact and grass over. It looked like a little burial mound in front of each hut.

There was a little kid playing in the front yard, but we didn't see him because he was on the other side of the bunker. When he heard us, he climbed to the top of the bunker to watch us go by. Unfortunately, he was carrying a toy gun. It was crude; it was made from the woody central rib of a palm leaf, but there was no doubt that it was intended to represent an AK-47. Our point caught the image in his peripheral vision, and he went into survival mode. Fortunately, he realized he was looking at a five-year-old and pulled the shot, so the child was just frightened, not cut in half. I knew in my bones that the next American unit that passed by the kid was dead. Not a doubt in my mind. So, to save his life, I took his toy away.

At that point in the war, we were supposed to be winning hearts and minds. The idea was to try to cut off support for the VC by convincing the locals that we were not, in fact, a brutal foreign army trying to prop up a corrupt puppet regime but actually the good guys from the land of peace and freedom trying to save them from the evil communists. So, I'm standing there trying to explain to the little boy's grandmother that I'm trying to save his life—in English. And she's spitting and yelling and kicking me in the shins with her bare feet and telling me what a rotten son of a bitch I am for trying to murder her grandchild—in Vietnamese. And I realized that if we needed hearts and minds to win the war, we didn't stand a chance. Grandma and I were having a very human misunderstanding that was absolutely unresolvable because we had no way to talk to each other. By trying to do the right thing, I had made a new VC sympathizer, and there wasn't a damned thing I could do about it. With the best intentions in the world, I could see this same scenario happening all over the country. The picture was even worse for those who did not have the best intentions. All too often, the refrain among field commanders was: "If you've got 'em by the balls, their hearts and minds will follow."

Lost & Real
Nick Butterfield

What good is a phantom leg
if only to remind you what you lost
and what is no longer a part of you,
a mere memory found inside the nervous
system that still sends signals to the brain
of what you once had.

All that is left is pitchfork pain and an untouchable itch.
Yet, you are a whole within a whole. What is
shattered can heal, but what is taken hides in
the shadows of what was.

You speak to ghosts because they are real
looking for a day dream to occupy the empty
space. The face behind the mask, bread before
the fire, life that really is death while the living
tell secrets.

Hunger when you have everything,
a lover when what you need is a friend. What you
need is truth-is why the words "In God We Trust"
are found in what you need. A soldier's
heart is broken only when you can't see what is
there and what is broke.

The uniform you wore and
left behind speaks to who you were. What is
found is more real than what you thought.

Faces

Jaime Lee Johnson

How does one accept the thought of, according to them, not having done their job? They showed up, did what they were told, went outside the wire, and met the locals … but never did their job.

How does one justify the thought that they felt cheated from doing their job when told to not return fire? It wasn't a training session or range, rounds were cracking overhead, and everyone knew where the fire was coming from.

Why does a soldier feel anger for never having destroyed the enemy with extreme prejudice? It's what we were trained for, they were there, we were ready, and the chance was taken from us.

How does one reconcile the contradictory emotions of being both outraged and elated that he does not have faces to haunt him?

Remembering Sandwich Lady
Bill Noyes

The land, the times, and the faces have undoubtedly changed with the years since 1969. Some may linger, recognizable still, but the youngest children that I knew are now aging adults, were I even to see them again. Their stories might add to the history I perceive but a lot has changed. The prettiest women, especially the older sandwich lady, my favorite with her big smile must already have passed from the living by now.

I might remember them as they were but also, I fear to learn their sadnesses brought on by the intervening years. Victory undoubtedly brought them these tears outside their control. The mountain might look the same, Nui Ba Den. The old French forts that were still there in the Ben Cui plantation when I trod those places are most likely gone now. The river has flowed past the town, Dau Tieng, many days since then.

Remembering must yield to all the changes that occur to things and places. Time will eventually replace the persistent but deficit past, though never completely.

Yesterday I awoke from a dream. I felt I could die. I was not choking but I sensed I might stop breathing. So, I breathed deeply and soon I was relieved to discover that I might return to a new day of living.

Was this dream the result of the war? My year-long fight to stay alive had been more than fifty years before. No panic but, also, no joy: merely the duty to return to living.

The other dreams that promptly followed my time at war have mostly morphed into tiresome replays of their battle scenes. They seem almost fictionalized now, and are quickly forgotten, or ignored. The dead still die again and the outcome stays the same. I could change the endings, I suppose, but I question to what purpose?

In those dreams cracks of bullets flying past were always startlingly loud. They can seem loud today but now appear farther away. They don't threaten instant death but the dead still do not rise again.

In one persistent dream I see the dead enemy soldier after the fight. Our battalion had fought his all night in June, 1969. I was the only one to see his position to my front. He was laying in the dirt in the morning, his buddies nearby. Was he brave but foolish I wondered? He'd got off a second shot before he died. Two of our guys in the squad next to ours were dead, I learned, because of his two RPGs.

I looked away when I saw that the cold morning dust had covered his eye. He was his mother's dream, to grow and watch her age. What of such dreams when victory finally came? Where must her dreams reside, to accommodate his achievement?

Dreams, and the hopes of the living, never die. They sail far above the storm until victorious sunlight can pierce the clouds. Then dreams can thrive in the quiet air. As surely as our lives are lit by dreams, and our dreams are our hope, the clouds will form from the ocean's waves and well up to shape this expectant world.

Sunny Day, Baghdad
Jaime Lee Johnson

On my way back from the hadji cafe and all is well. For once, I actually take a moment to look around and appreciate where I am, but it didn't last long.

As I walk back to my room where my best friend is sleeping, an officer comes my way. I say, "Good afternoon, sir." and carry on, but he had other plans. He stopped me and asked why I didn't salute him. I said, "Sniper check, sir." He didn't like that and said we're in the green zone and any nearby buildings have been cleared. We went back and forth, but eventually I did salute him.

I stood at attention and raised my right hand, but it all felt like it was in slow motion in a movie where something bad was going to happen.

Heels together with fingertips touching the brim of my cover, I repeat my earlier greeting. He returns the salute and I await the pink mist I tried to prevent. Time has slowed even more. I ask myself, "Is this it? Is this going to be the first friendly I see killed and right in front of me?"

He lowers his salute and walks away. I stand there, waiting for the pink mist and the crack of the shot to follow. I wait, and wait, and wait. But it never comes.

I return to my previous task, but now with a feeling of astonishment and frustration of the stupidity I just experienced as I mutter to myself, "You lucky piece of shit."

Lost Leg I
G. Craige Edgerton

Whump, whump, whump, whump.

The 3-ton helicopter climbs up from the valley below, rotors whirring. Seeking a broken warrior, his leg fodder for the jungle. The corpsman, who can't legally buy booze, performs almost like God, trying to repair the broken Marine.

Whump, whump, whump, whump.

The chopper ascends closer to the firebase, bringing the Marine health, home, honor, or, just maybe, family horror.

Whump, Whump, Whump, Whump.

Louder the beast climbs, searching the LZ while the pilot, remembering his own son graduating high school this week, dreads picking up another youngster his son's age.

WHUMP, WHUMP, WHUMP, WHUMP

Dust flies and ponchos cover the stump of a leg. *"PREPARE TO EVACUATE"*

WHUMP, WHUMP, WHUMP, WHUMP

Chaos, dirt, screaming directions by hand, *will my son go to college with this boy* the pilot surmises. The PFC, in foggy recollection, *Will*

*I see the World again? Will I make it? Will I...*as he fades into unconsciousness. The pilot, with a thumbs up, whisks the Marine away. Is this the last ride for him? Will his leg be a memory like the son he will never know?

Lost Leg II
G. Craige Edgerton

For 54 years, I've thought about that Marine. I was the one directing the evacuation. It is etched in my memory as though it were yesterday. The leg dangled from the knee, the corpsman trying to save it. I was new to the country and had no training in directing an evacuation, but I was a Second Lieutenant and was assigned the duty.

Yes, it was gruesome. The agony of the Marine and the chaos of the chopper wash were almost too much to endure. But I learned that you dig down, do what you think is best, and hope that you are right.

After loading and securing the Marine, the chopper dove into the jungle-covered canyon below and disappeared. I returned to my assigned duties and tried to forget about the legless Marine. But I couldn't. The questions about what happened to him slid to the back of my mind and periodically emerged randomly for the next 54 years.

Did he die in that chopper? Did he die in a hospital in Tokyo? Did he survive and get back to the World? Was he able to reunite with his girlfriend and eventually get married? Had the girlfriend moved on to another? Did he use booze and drugs to mitigate the pain, not only of the lost leg but of guilt and remorse and finally losing that girl who had waited for him to return? Did he have that son? And if so, did he ever really know him, or were both lost to the pain he suffered? Was he injured so badly that he was unable to have a son?

Did he accept his tragedy of war and move on with his life, his prosthetic a constant companion? Was the girl of his dreams waiting to share a life together as they raised a family of successful children and a gaggle of grandchildren? Did he find meaning in his lost leg and dedicate his life to helping others? Is he still alive out there somewhere wondering about that Lieutenant who helped him onto that chopper that June day in 1969?

I have no idea how to answer any of these questions. That is one of the unrecognized tragedies of war. **The not knowing**. That Marine will always be a part of me, of my experience of war. I never knew his name or saw his face. I just saw that dangling leg and the chopper that tried to save him.

Now, I write about this for myself, for my recovery, but also for others who want to know what war is like and why it is so hard for so many to open up and talk about their experiences. Most importantly, I write about this for that Marine that I will never know. The tragedy of war doesn't leave those of us who were there. We try to forget, but most of us are unsuccessful.

Today, I live a very peaceful, successful, and fulfilling life with a great family and community that provides me with challenges that allow me to grow and time in my twilight years to reflect on a good life. So, don't feel sorry for me. Viet Nam was one of many experiences; thankfully, it did not define me. For many, many years, I would not admit that I was in Vietnam and certainly not admit that I was a Marine in combat. But now I can. Not with pride or anger or any other emotion. But just another fact of my life. I was there, I did my best, I served, and I came home.

I want the reader to understand why vets won't talk to you. One aspect is the not knowing, and they don't know how to answer. It is not clear to them how to talk about it. There are too many unknowns. The memories can be ghostlike, unseen, floating all around them all the time even though they are not consciously aware of them. So be patient with them. With a little encouragement and guidance, possibly from the Vet Center, healing just might follow.

From the Back of the Truck, How I Remember Vietnam I

Doug Nelson

We were known to the Vietnamese people by our army trucks, as well as by our helicopters. I saw a child in Saigon playing in the street, making engine sounds, and sitting in a cardboard box with a flap of the box folded down in front like an army truck windshield. The Army three-quarter-ton truck in those days looked caught in a time warp between WWI and WWII. It had high rounded fenders and torpedo-shaped headlights on either side of a hood tapering to the front. The cargo bed had wood slat sides and bench seats. Five of us were riding in the back of the truck.

Vietnam, between Saigon and the Cambodian border, was hot in December, especially by about nine in the morning. Vietnam had an unmistakable odor from a large population with a third-world sewage system. Ditches ran through neighborhoods and along roads. People simply used the ditch. Our trucks were in line, moving very slowly, sharing the road with motorcycles and motorcycle-driven tiny trucks with elongated and widened bodies that carried people, pigs, bundles of chickens bound together by their feet, and belongings tied up in cloth. The dry, choking dust flew in swirls, covering everyone on the road.

The other four soldiers were in my unit, co-workers, guys whose approval I valued because I had to live and work with them. On the floor were several care packages, cartons of candy, cigarettes, matches, toothpaste, and soap. We tossed the gum and candy to the children and watched, amused, as they scrambled after their brightly colored wrappers.

Two of my buddies began throwing large bars of soap

progressively harder at people along the road, those riding bicycles, walking, and carrying bundles on their heads. I giggled nervously, not wanting to try to correct the behavior of buddies of the same rank and status as I.

We passed a Vietnamese man who could have been between forty and seventy, lean, wiry, brown. Compared to us, he was old. He was balancing on his shoulders, suspended from a thick yoke of wood, two large rusty cans of water, joined to the ends of his yoke by rusty wire and heavy twine.

When a full-sized bar of Ivory soap was thrown at him, he dodged and, in doing so, looked up at me, not at the big red-haired soldier who threw the soap. I expected to see hate in his eyes. What I saw was the look of an older brother or a disapproving father. It said, "You laugh at this, do you? You know better, I think."

As the big guy took the final major league windup with the last big chunk of soap, our truck slowed in traffic, and the old man caught up to us, carrying his burden. He saw the final windup and the brick of soap coming at him and turned to balance himself so that the wooden yoke lay across his shoulders, his arms outstretched. Something was disturbingly familiar about the outstretched arms, his gauntness, and his downcast face.

No more candy or soap was thrown, but only because we had no more. I can tell you, though, that not one of us ever spoke of the incident. We all knew we were wrong. As a young man, I was unwilling even to pay the price of the disapproval of my buddies. I tried to talk to Jim, my closest friend, about it. All he said was, "We've been over here too long. It's makin' us crazy. You're bein' too hard on yourself. It's a good thing we're this short."

I have heard stories I don't doubt are true about incidents like shooting at water buffalo from trucks or helicopters or even at people working in their fields. What might we have done if we had been in a more isolated place, with little or no supervision? Might we have behaved as pillagers, plunderers, and worse throughout human history?

From the Back of the Truck, How I Remember Vietnam II
Doug Nelson

I was raised as a Protestant Christian, making peep boxes in Vacation Bible School with cutouts of Mary, Joseph, and the donkey in the shoebox. One end was covered in orange cellophane so that peeping through a hole in the other end, I'd see them walking into the sunset.

What you are taught as a child does not leave you. As a thinking young person, you question everything, a healthy part of growing up. However, you also cling to the thought that within what you were taught, there must be some profound truth at the core of your spiritual teaching that might be true and incorruptible.

Although I have discarded some Judeo-Christian teachings as scientifically or logically absurd, I am left with this parable in metaphor, this image. As an older adult, I think of Christ down in the dusty road, looking up at us, arms outstretched on the Cross, from the filth, from among the people we thought we despised.

I think that he is more likely to look at us from among those fleeing from war, among the victims of our smart bombs, among the homeless, hungry, lame, and broken-hearted. I think he (or, for that matter, she) is as likely to look up at us as down upon us, but always staring us in the eye and looking into our hearts.

This vision will not leave me. The Iraqi man at Abu Ghraib prison stands with arms outstretched, connected to electrical wires. If he looks at us, it is through the threads of a blindfold. Still, he looks. Children and their parents in Rafah lie broken to pieces, bloody rags in the muddy streets, the consequences of American industry, brokered to the people of Israel for the "defense" of their country.

The concept of sin is a prevalent one in the Judeo-Christian tradition and is found also in Islam. It is a philosophically and practically useful idea. It can explain the presence of evil in a world we believe to be overseen by a loving and just God. More importantly, it throws the responsibility for "sin" onto us as individuals. The facts are that we were in a war we didn't want to be in, that our country is made up of flawed institutions, and that believers in any religious tradition are often our own worst witnesses. The facts do not relieve us of personal responsibility for our actions or lack of action. We sin when we act and speak in such a way that our fellow man is injured, however slightly, by what we've done and when we act purely out of self-interest and desire with no thought of consequences.

What was in the old man's buckets – the sin of our despicable behavior on the one side and the sin of someone who knew better on the other, yet who allowed his friends to inflict suffering and did nothing? Perhaps the other side of sin, in addition to our thoughtless or cruel actions, is in his second bucket: our failure to address injustice, hate, and unjustified war.

We who are fortunate enough to have the benefit of some education talk in abstract terms of "society" or "culture" and make pronouncements about what is wrong with "it." We feel superior. We fool ourselves into thinking that the fault lies somewhere outside ourselves. In doing so, we can let ourselves off the hook of personal responsibility.

From the Back of the Truck, How I Remember Vietnam III
Doug Nelson

The older generation in our country seems to share this notion that the war experience is somehow "character-building." Every generation needs to participate in America's greatness, manifest destiny, exceptionalism, or whatever they want to call our penchant for war. I remember wearing an army helmet for the first time and realizing that my father had worn the same helmet shape, and that my thin face was as equally lost beneath it as was his.

When we are at war, or when the powers that be in our country are trying to gather support for war, we find "those other people" portrayed in parts of the press, in popular culture and even in public political discourse as subhuman, as lacking in some basic human qualities. At a Protestant chapel retreat during my army job training, I was told that the Vietnamese did not value human life as we do, that the Viet Cong were the forces of evil, and that God was on our side. Today, what other people do we now claim "do not value human life"?

I thought I knew better. As a child, I found a Nazi belt buckle among my Dad's mementos with the inscription, "Gott Mit Uns." We see Christ in our own image. He is "with" us partly because we think he looks like us. We are so sure that he doesn't look Asian, African, or, curiously, even Middle Eastern. We only need to look at European religious art in any museum. The Middle Eastern nose is the only concession we want to make to the fact of historical, ethnic origin.

We are regaled as children by Hebraic myths of the Chosen People, justified in their defense of themselves but also in their seizure of the lands of other populations. Anyone who dared to keep them in slavery incurred the wrath of the one true God in the form of floods, plagues, and the loss of their children. It has been all too easy for us to borrow or steal this scriptural justification from other people in another time, see ourselves as "chosen people," and then extend this to the notion of our "exceptionalism."

The "us versus them" idea was not original to the ancient Hebrew people. Ethnological studies show that many human cultures have seen themselves as opposed to the rest of the world as they knew it. Their names for themselves often directly translate to such names as "The People," with everyone else being just "those other people."

I think that this religion-driven self-righteousness is what makes it possible to justify the use of torture, atomic weapons, drones, cluster bombs, napalm, white phosphorus, Agent Orange, and depleted uranium. To inflict this pain and suffering on other people, we must somehow see them as less than human, their lives as of less value than those of our fellow soldiers, and their love for their children as somehow less than our love for ours.

My buddies and I didn't want to be in Vietnam. We hated being there in the stinking heat and, by extension, acted as if we hated the people of that unfortunate country for "misbehaving" in such a way that our government felt compelled to send us there.

We have now seen the news film footage of Iraqis suspected of being "insurgents," with an American soldier standing with his foot on a man's neck. In the past twenty years, we have more frequently seen the sight of Americans being detained by our own police, pinned to the ground by a knee to the back or neck, or abused with force completely unjustified by the offense. Any of us might be treated as the "enemy," as inmates, or, if you will, as "those other people." The college psychology experiment continues to go very wrong. This is what the rest of the world sees when they see America. If they are honest, they will see us as no better than themselves in the darker parts of their own histories.

From the Back of the Truck, How I Remember Vietnam IV

Doug Nelson

What is the price of "doing the right thing," of caring more about decency and justice than about how our buddies might view us? Army Specialist Joe Darby paid a dear price for doing the right thing. His unit, the 372nd Military Police Company, was a National Guard unit sent to Iraq, inadequately trained and poorly led. Joe Darby had seen enough of the abuse of Iraqi detainees at Abu Ghraib prison and, in 2004, reported what he knew to be going on. His own hometown has expressed disgust at and disapproval of his actions. We cannot talk with him because he is sequestered away for his own safety. He must know that he is respected by people he will never meet. He needs to hear, "You did well, son."

Warrant Officer Hugh Thompson landed his observation helicopter in My Lai, Vietnam in 1968 to try to put a stop to the killing of civilians by a US Army infantry platoon. A US senator told him that the only person who should be punished for My Lai was he, the only one who had taken the initiative to stop the killing and had reported it to authorities.

Might we pay a price for doing as we were told, for seeking the approval of others? More typically, young men (and now women) have been scarred simply by complying with orders. Today, the operators of drones, who sit in air-conditioned offices and who kill using a screen and a computer, are experiencing the symptoms of moral scarring as post-traumatic stress disorder.

As a veterans' services counselor for twelve years, I've had veterans of all our wars open up to me. An old man tearfully told me how he sees the faces of the mother and children he killed when he heard rustling noises in the dark corner of a hut in Vietnam and fired a burst from his rifle. An Iraq veteran told me of Iraqi parents killed in cars, the children screaming in the back seat, covered with the brains and blood of their parents, because their dad had misinterpreted our soldiers' hand signals at a traffic checkpoint.

Hard to take, is it? We should be glad it's hard to take. If you believe in God, then praise Him (or Her) that it is hard to take. It is hard to take because we have consciences because we know that the Vietnamese, the Iraqis, the Afghans, the Israelis, and the Yemeni are God's children, just like us. Jesus said as much; there are no chosen people.

Are we Americans too accustomed to war? Must WWII be a paradigm for all of our foreign relations decisions? Do we continue to regale our sons with stories of courage under fire and Medals of Honor?

My father went to war, volunteering with his buddies for the infantry when he was bored with life in a posh ordnance unit. He would not talk in detail with me about combat, even after I had returned from Vietnam. But when I had dropped out of college and told my parents that I intended to enlist in the army to avoid infantry service in the draft, he called me to the kitchen table soon after dinner and warned me about going to this war. "This one doesn't look right to me. I don't think we have any business over there. Those people never did anything to us. Go to an easier college, get back in school." He was a soldier; I would be also. I ignored his warning and ended up in 'Nam. Dad died in 1996. How interesting and ironic that WWII veterans were among the veterans who welcomed me to Veterans For Peace in 2003.

I hope my war story raises questions, since it does not seem to answer any. What would I have done if faced with my unit's participation in My Lai or Abu Ghraib?

We Americans believe our political and social systems are the culmination of Western civilization's assertions of people's right to self-determination by way of a representative government.

However, our founding fathers and other prominent thoughtful Americans have warned of the excessive influence of private interests, of overemphasis on security to the point of paranoia, and of an economy and a society geared to perpetual war. We have so far failed on every count and, additionally, now allow public discourse to resemble a schoolyard brawl. Is addressing the issue at hand, with points made and examples offered, so difficult? Will we allow this societal chaos to lead us blundering into still another war, for vague purposes and against an undefined enemy?

If our very own sons were subject to a draft, in addition to the sons of "those other people," would we then speak out? If others we see as decent moral people happen to believe in the righteousness of a foreign policy calling for war, how do we love them as brothers and sisters and not compromise our opposition to war?

If we have not already sold our pathetic semblance of democracy to the highest bidders, we may have some choice over whom we entrust to decide such questions as whether or not we go to war. Or we can stand idly by and empower our leaders to put another generation in the backs of army trucks. In 1941, many thousands of young German men rode away to the East in their trucks, never to see home again. They thought they were exceptional. Do not think for a minute that we are exceptional. We are not.

Nothing Special
Bill Noyes

Going to war, for an individual, should be regarded as a kind of spirit quest. It can become destructive personally but it also will be instructive spiritually. The lesson is not confined to a soldier's time in combat since those events may well last, by their results or mentally, far into his future. It is a challenging experience for him, avoided by most people and shunned for the threat it poses, while it captivates everyone's attention.

The effects and the results of war can't be averted. They are too profound. The impact extends far beyond the few participants in war. It lasts throughout history. Accordingly, many heroes come from our wars, though no singular or definitive traits can trace the virtue to be found in war experiences.

Opposites will benefit from their experiences at war, while their contrary feats and motivations need not insure eithers' survival. Real actions yield flexible interpretations. The truth of the moment when it's gone somehow establishes a solid basis for our thoughts. We reach and grasp instinctively toward a spiritual plane through war.

One's war experience can be a long ordeal or a quick death, but it is never a blasé spiritual awareness. The emotion released in the spiritual blast that is war and its aftermath far exceeds the obvious question of survival. Indeed, the dead may seem the fortunate, who have all their questions about life answered quickly. The state of war can answer many important questions concerning courage and personal ability, but it presents greater questions that can linger in our minds. These questions may have no possible answer during the war and require decades of thought and living to finally conclude. War strips away the fabric that obscures the basic purpose of life, and its revelations are gained only after this price is paid.

Each soldier carries more into battle than himself in many ways, but especially spiritually. While many have much at stake in his performance, his victory or loss, spiritually, involves a contrary result for another. Why it must be so is the answer that spirit seeks. War brings this problem to each soldier but his answer, for many years, may elude his grasp. Every experience he carries away from battle has a background of failures which he must remember if he is to appreciate his success. War is a spiritual experimentation for soldiers, equal to any scientific trial.

Six months into my year at war, I returned to our camp after a sleepless night on a three-man listening post. It was early morning, and I anticipated riding as the 50cal gunner so that I could nap during movements. My squad's APC was being repaired so we would ride on another squad's vehicle. As we clambered aboard, because that squad had sent a man on an ambush patrol that night and because he could not be left behind as a bunker guard to sleep, he demanded the restful gunner job. We nearly fought for the privilege but I relented, knowing the job would be unattractive if that day we became involved in a heavy fight. I chose to walk as machine gunner at the head of our road sweep going away from our patrol base.

After our sweep patrol, our platoon of three APCs set up an outpost position to secure the road until the convoy would pass later in the day. The position was located where several convoy ambushes had occurred months and years past. It was not a place unfamiliar to me since I'd patrolled in the past through the shattered and destroyed bunkers and fighting holes. Now, as I watched and saw nothing next to my machine gun, I wondered what interesting relics might be found by a patient search of the area. The platoon of about twenty-five waited under constructed shade at each position under the hot sun since any trees had been previously shot away.

I decided to go look. Leaving the heavy machine gun in place, I chose not to return to the track for a rifle. Then I stepped forward and onto an old paddy dike where I stood wondering. "Should I proceed?" I carried two grenades in my pockets in case I was surprised.

The rest of the outposted soldiers bantered and lollygagged to my sides and rear as I stood waiting. The sun burned, and a slight breeze blew as I worried that it might be unsafe to go further. I listened and thought as if searching for signs, but without knowing what I must see.

Suddenly, I felt an inaudible presence high above and to my right. "It doesn't matter!" without sound, and I looked, but it had gone. I felt I'd been told to decide because time could not stay suspended. Go forward or back, it didn't matter, but I must act.

I returned to my previous concern. Then I sensed, beside the strange presence, that I was being watched from my front. Someone was looking intently at me standing there. I decided that it was prudent not to test the moment. Two grenades might be of no help soon. So, I stepped back off the dike and returned to my squad position.

A little later, the convoy appeared and rumbled down the road past our platoon. The last truck passed as we loaded onto our three tracks and waited. We would receive directions by radio to go on another mission somewhere else. The convoy was nearing the culvert and little stream near the Ben Cui plantation, where the rest of the company was out-posted.

Rattling machine guns started there, with explosions. The gunshots swept like a wave to the front of our platoon. We leaped to the ground as bullets flew past. The enemy fire did not let up for fifteen minutes or more. We each shot back from within depressions or behind stumps.

Our 50cal gunners were individually shot away, or they abandoned their guns. Only our track still fired bursts throughout this time. That was the gun where I might have fought had I stayed to serve it. I shot my machine gun in short bursts from a depression to the rear of the track, but it afforded little cover. I'd fired most of my basic load when I decided to conserve the last two belts: two hundred rounds. My position and our situation were becoming desperate, and I might have to move.

I listened as the enemy fire slackened. I searched for answers why and decided they must be down in their holes reloading. When they came up to fire again, some of them would charge the tracks. I had no choice but to move now. I would get as close to their holes as possible and shoot into the top inches to kill or discourage them. Looking down the barrel of my gun, with each step, I shot two or three rounds into the targets I could recognize. Little fire seemed coming from our men in support of my assault.

When I gained the front of our track, I felt protected to that side, so I swept right at the front of the next two tracks. An enemy was crawling forward nearby and he got two bursts. Then the belt was finished and I kneeled to reload my last belt. I swept back, three rounds in each burst, and I was again shooting to my front. The last belt was gone and I retreated quickly to get more ammo.

At the back of our track, I discovered the driver kneeling with a head wound. I ripped open my one bandage to apply but he motioned into the open door. When I looked I saw the 50cal gunner lying on the ammo cans with a fountain of blood spurting from his head. I gave the driver the bandage to apply himself as I leapt into the APC.

He would have only moments to live if he continued to bleed, so I covered the wound with one hand and held his head up with the other. Quickly, I realized that I could do no more. Nor could I release him without his imminent death. I had become as trapped as he in this final moment of life. I could only hope that the enemy would not blow the track, or appear at the door.

Minutes passed, and finally, two squad mates helped move the wounded gunner out of the track. After some time, the company medic administered fluids and took the gunner to where he could be put on a medivac chopper, but he died flying into the base camp. The battle continued through the rest of the day, but in our platoon area, the enemy was already defeated.

I had no idea what to make of this day's experience. New men soon appeared in the squads to replace the many we lost, but there is no downtime in war because no one generally volunteers to share your time in danger. Operations proceed; schedules are met with half the manpower, and the inconsequential battles are documented as if they are important. I told no one about the voice that was not there.

But it angered me that this spirit did not bother to warn me about what would soon come. It had a schedule it wished to keep, and it held no concern for me, that I could see. That anger could only further explode with each added day of experience in this lost war. The spirit didn't care. Or, I began to ponder, did spirit just know far more than could I about such things?

A month later, I was officially presented with an award for that day's battle: a silver star at Fire Support Base Wood2. The citation made a big deal about saving a dying man but very little about assaulting the enemy. I was never told who wrote the thing up. It seemed they had things turned around militarily, but it was just a further lesson about the fallacy of awards. Ribbons are merely cheap tools for Napoleon and all militias. They are really of little worth to most soldiers. That day would not be my closest to, nor last brush with death.

After the war, after the trials of adjustment to again join a more civil but less fair social existence, I joined an early vet group. It was positively, openly prejudicial toward those with experience in combat arms. With time I learned that this Vietnam Combat Veterans was no more than a scam toward those who held such prejudices. The group leaders profited from and degraded, accordingly, their members by using this lever against them. I moved on. With more exposure to a variety of veterans, I could begin to see that many others can have legitimate needs, and they, too, deserve recognition for their service. Their emotional trials could be as big a part of their experience as any veteran of combat.

In particular, I bumped into an ex-sailor on a Zoom program I frequented. He was a Navy veteran and a Merchant Marine seaman of long experience. His coherence and compositional ability were extraordinary, and he told of the importance of handrails on board ships. Especially at sea, in storms in many ways, they become the metal life lines for sailors in so many ways. He made the case that such sturdy and tangible devices could serve all people who might seem washed away by emotional storms or social isolation. What great insight and clarity he presented in his exposition of how handrails had aided him! From his service experience follows, the crucial nature of handrails.

The solid, sturdy handrails bring the seaman up from the depths of the ship when it is his time to rejuvenate on deck. Without rails, the vertical ladders are nearly impossible to climb. They work in the darkest of times, bringing him from the doldrums of despair to the fresh and open space above. Even in the worst sea, they serve to stop him from being swept away and are sturdy, familiar, and trusted to hold. They are the touch he needs, his opportunity to view the vast and wondrous ocean and sky in the world all around. He gains confidence and reassurance that when he must again return to his labor below deck, he can anticipate his eventual return to freedom above.

Meeting others since the war and thinking constantly about experiences, I began to see how spirit works. Change began to happen in me and how I saw things. Even the anger I felt from the war became less. There was no sudden shock to this awareness, no final answer, only tiny shifts in my perspective. Spirit didn't set any bushes ablaze or part any water because that would take attention away from the answers I sought. Daily events sufficed to form new understanding.

Change can happen, must happen, to give spirit its due. We grasp what handrails we can find in the dark and are brought up. When we've climbed above, we must still look at our world before appreciating what's seen. Ours is an active world, and it is not meant to stay still. Nor is it meant to remain as we think it should be or have found it to be. It must always change. Each change is meant to be.

Life changes happen slowly, generally. Only in modern warfare do we expect that killed soldiers will be vaporized and instantly disappear. In the war, I watched a dead man disappear for more than a month. Flies came; maggots grew and devoured the flesh. The mass collapsed into the ground, and the crumbling continued. Other creatures hatched and grew. Finally animals carried off most of the bones. It always takes time, and nature depends on this process.

Even the Big Bang was no more than the beginning of a long, natural evolution of things to come. I percolate the coffee or steep the tea, but my spirit enjoys the flavor through my tasting and the friendships I pursue. There is, of course, nothing special about a particular beverage. But there is always more to events than what we may notice or see. Results seem to be the purpose for change, but the reward may be the effort itself, making perfect achievement less important.

Smells of Neville

G. Craige Edgerton

Deep in the jungle
On a shaved-top hill
Firebase Neville, Vietnam
My combat home.

The scorching sun
And a harsh wind
Bring foul smoke
From kerosene burnt latrines.

The clay scent
Of the floor in my hooch
Akin to my home garden
Always wet and earthy

Chopper fuel
Mixed with backwash.
Sticking to my nostrils
Recurring in my dreams

Ham and lima beans
C-rations simmer.
The aroma stifles my appetite.
I'm losing too much weight.

Evening cool breezes
Jungle fragrances
As nighttime flora emerges.
Relief from the steamy jungle.

It's the scent,
The smells that take me back.
Firebase Neville, Vietnam
My combat home.

Denied

Jaime Lee Johnson

O900 hours and we're on the clock. Vehicles fueled, radios checked, spare ammo stowed away, then I check my own gear.

1000 hours. Nothing.

1015 hours. I hear running on the rocks and then a pounding on my door before I hear "QRF" yelled and in an instant, I'm out of bed and in full kit. Just as I was getting into my HMMWV, I hear the squad leader yell, "Stand down. QRF canceled."

1100 hours and it's my turn on radio watch. I hear miscellaneous traffic and do a radio check. Time slows as I intently listen for the call.

1300 hours and I'm relieved by my replacement, but not a few seconds after getting back to my room when I hear the familiar sound of the running on rocks.

1305 hours and we're driving out of the motorpool when I get the call to stand down. We turn around, park the vehicles, and strip off our gear.

1400 hours and I'm still amped up. I walk around the motorpool to cool off. I see others doing the same.

1640 hours and the third call comes in. This time, I get a feeling that this is the one. We load up, roll out, and this time we get all the way out the gate before we're told to stand down again. The HMMWV goes from being filled with the sounds of excitement to groans of frustration.

1645 hours and we're back at the motorpool. I see faces of anger and hear the occasional yell of colorful comments about the wasted time. I was just as bad, if not worse. I yelled out, "Let us do our fucking jobs!" before heading off to chow for the rest of the shift.

You Decide
B 2/22, 11 March 1969
Bill Noyes

I know where this story is going. How must it be told? I ask, why even tell such a curious tale? As an artist, I feel challenged, but as a man, I still wonder why. So, first, I lay my pen down as I try to remember the lack of sound at that exact time on that fateful day. Remembering nothing! It's a daunting trick. But then I realize every story is exactly such a thing before the words are put to paper and its form is cast in stone.

It is always the same challenge and must be met in the same way. I feel free to go where I did not go then, when another step might have brought me there, to the oblivion that I seek.

The first shots began far away where the passing convoy had gone. Then it rolled in crescendo until, in a moment, our front erupted when the bullets split our air. The long ambush had started, to our complete surprise, as we leaped from atop our tracks to the dusty ground. We hid there in the dust and grass, a platoon of startled soldiers. We hid in fear, beginning to fight for our lives.

We were quickly bloodied, in legs while running for the little cover, in backs and heads while serving our heavy weapons. Well concealed snipers picked off the easy targets as we dared to locate their general positions. This early battle was not going well for our platoon.

The rest of our company and the distant convoy were beyond our concern. Our fight was to our immediate front, and behind. I lay pressed into a shallow depression, by the searing sun, and by the crack of bullets just above me. My hearing focused on the bullet's flight in order to guess the direction of the shooter, where I would try to deliver each answering burst. The chatter of our fire was matched by theirs. My bursts continued until my ammunition was about half gone.

I lay in my quandary and pondered my fate. Listening, I looked when I dared; I heard the clatter of our fire and theirs'. I sensed only one of our heavy machine guns still answered their fire. Some of our rifles still spat back at their bursts. So, worried anticipation stalked my mind, for I knew my shallow cover would yield its safety if the enemy chose to assault, firing from a higher angle.

I might not have long. Listening intently, I tried to figure out what they might do next, when I realized the enemy fire had slackened. Except for a couple of our rifles, an eerie quiet had descended over our battleground.

My guess was that they were down in their holes, reloading magazines for an assault. I might have little time left. I decided to rise and began advancing from my poor cover at the rear of our track, toward its front. I would then have a clear shot at the enemy as each came up from their hole to assault.

With each step I fired three rounds at any suspected position. I had the track on my left for protection until I reached its front. My short belt of about sixty rounds was used up and I reloaded my last hundred round belt. Though there were no others up and little fire from our rifles, the enemy stayed down in their holes, or died there from my bursts, except for one who was likely crawling forward with an RPG.

I peppered each target along the platoon front. Three rounds went into each potential hole until my last belt was gone. I retreated toward the back of the track to get more ammo or to switch to my M16. The battle continued much longer past this point and two other companies joined the fight. They each lost people too, and many enemies died that day. I suppose the result of this particular fight didn't matter much in the war, but I pondered the voice, that I hadn't heard before the battle, for many years. Was the inconclusiveness of war really the only point, that the ghoul with no voice had to offer me?

It made me very angry, the more I thought about it. Had I gone forward, as I almost did that day, perhaps I'd have been the first to die, and thereby learned the secret of life. Shouldn't a spirit who must reveal itself, after all, at least offer some positive direction concerning such a great opportunity?

But I digress. Let me go back in this story to the time before the shooting started. It could be told as an over complicated tale, but I'll try to make it simple. The day's events in complicated fashion follow this simple rule, that action reveals truth.

After our morning sweep of 239er for mines, our platoon had set up an outpost there to await the passing of the convoy and to secure its route. It was an often used ambush location and I'd patrolled through the area a number of times. I'd taken note of the refuse of battle in the past. Broken machine gun wheels, scattered casings, and left scattered debris amidst fighting bunkers, but I'd never taken the time to look through it.

On this hot March day I felt bored waiting by my machine gun, so eventually decided to go to the old battleground to our front and explore. There might be some war souvenir, or a chieu hoi leaflet laying in the dust for the taking. We had been there for a while and no one had noticed any sign of the enemy, so, though I should take a weapon, the machine gun being too heavy, I decided to go with only the grenades in my pockets.

Everyone else was relaxing under poncho liners or eating, so a few paces brought me alone to the old paddy dike that separated our position from the torn tangle of bushes and thorns where the old bunkers lay. I stopped at the dike and thought this would not be the first time a guy was shot while seeking a private pee. Then I stepped onto the dike and waited. I searched the tangled bushes for any sign, to be sure.

Was this a good time? Was this the wrong time? I waited standing there suspended in time. I searched for an answer as if in prevarication, but I waited as my mind probed the unknown. Nothing moved, nor did the wind stir as I felt someone's presence. Was I being watched, awaiting my next step? Should I have my rifle?

I was startled by a voice, close, but high above me and inaudible. I heard, "It does not matter!" and I knew by implication that I must act. There was nothing when I looked toward the sky, no vanishing cloud nor flash of something. Neither question nor an answer could follow when it was gone.

I returned to the question as to my next step in life. I could sense someone intently watching; almost feel his obsession with my presence before him. "What the hell was that?" I questioned, then opted for prudence and returned to my gun. War trophy acquisition would be put off till another time.

It was not long after that, that the convoy rumbled past us. So, as the last trucks rolled on their way to Dau Tieng we were ordered to mount up and prepare to leave our position. We all thought we'd have a busy day before us, somewhere else.

Depression and Suicide
Jim Marney-Petix

We came on the village about an hour before first light. At a clump of palm trees, I posted two riflemen and a radio operator to guard our rear. The rest of the platoon moved into position to search the village. About the time we were in place, I got a call from my rear guard that someone was walking up the trail. Now the whole country was under dusk to dawn curfew, so anyone moving around at this hour could be assumed to be an enemy soldier. Also, if he's walking up on the rear of my platoon, I can't afford to care what he is—if he makes a noise, he'll get us killed. I told the guards to take care of it—quietly. The sweep through the village didn't turn up a damned thing. Best we could tell the Viet Cong we were looking for left at least an hour before we arrived. The guy walking up our rear was actually a girl lying on the ground with her throat cut. She was four months pregnant. We didn't care—she was VC; she was carrying a VC cadet.

Combat is not like real life. A man who's adjusted to combat is a psychotic killer by civilian standards. I saw people as dangerous objects and killed them with no more thought than killing a mosquito. That was the way it had to be, otherwise I would never have been able to do my job. And all my training from boot camp on was designed specifically to get me to that point. The problem was that when it was all over, I was dumped back into the world without any training to make me a human again. For a while, my military training could justify my wartime experiences. But gradually, my attitudes and values changed, and five years later, I was a civilian again. Unfortunately, the memories were still there. Everything I saw, everything I did, everything I thought during the war was now seen through civilian eyes. I found myself trapped in the same body with someone I despised. All I wanted to do was die.

Ode to the Unknown Warrior
G. Craige Edgerton

I don't know your name,
or what country you are from,
or what language you speak,
or what era you battled.

But I know what you did.

You attained the apex of humanity,
Giving up yourself for your fellow human.
Your deeds were not recorded,
And the sacrifices of you and your compatriots
Will forever remain unknown.

But I know what you did.

No headlines in the hometown paper,
no plaque near the local park,
no remembrance of what you did that day.
But the impact is engraved
in the tableau of unwritten history,
the history of man's humanity to man.

And I know what you did.

Your bravery, or courage, or valor,
Your fear or anger or terror,
Are all wrapped in your memories
Some hidden, not to be shared.
Others shared, not to be hidden.

But I know what you did. . .
. . .because I, too, was there.

Hostile Fire Pay
R. Marshall Burgamy

"FORE!" "FORE RIGHT!", I called out as the well-struck drive off my new Titlest T2 Driver slipped from an easy fade to a full blown slice on the 5th hole of Green Hills Country Club, not far from San Francisco International Airport. I had come a long way since serving with the United States Marine Corps in VietNam. I had put it behind me, or mostly so I thought, returning to college, going to grad school, attempting law school, even a tour with the Peace Corps before teaching university from the Northeast in the US, to Malaysia, Kuwait and Costa Rica, finally ending up at the University of San Francisco. Always on the move.

As I walked toward my ball in the other fairway chatting amicably with the younger golfers, fellow club members all, a loud boom from the airport sent me diving to the deck. The guys were a bit startled to see me go down, and nervously chuckled, not knowing quite what to say. Trying to regain a modicum of dignity, I got up, made some lame excuse about being jumpy at loud noises, and we all pretended nothing really out of the ordinary had happened. They graciously moved on as I went to my ball.

It was then, that once again, it all came raging back to me from that night of October, 1969; me jumping to my feet, startled by the salty Staff Sergeant's dive to the floor of our hooch at Dong Ha Combat Base a few miles from the DMZ; The Marine Dead Zone, as it became known. I still see the wild look in his eyes, jungle boots thrust in the air as he hit the deck across from my fold-out field desk. We were busy making entries into most of the Third Marine Division's pay records; assiduously cranking hand-operated adding machines, typing on Remington manual typewriters. There were thousands of entries to be made as men and materiale were being moved around that Fall of 1969. Nixon had promised to bring the boys home, and we were unwittingly complicit in his mendacious and sinister move; pawns in a political playbook we would only become fully aware of much later.

We were building bogus units of short-timers (those whose 13 month combat tour was near end), who would rotate back to the "World", as we called the US, where they would be ceremoniously paraded through the streets, as if, the troops were coming home, as if we were ending our military occupation of South VietNam. The rest of us, with time remaining, were being moved to other units in VietNam, or to Okinawa, where many of us would return to VietNam "on float," aboard Navy ships.

Until that point in my enlistment with the Marine Corps, adding Hostile Fire Pay to thick yellow pay records was a perfunctory task learned at Basic Disbursing School in Camp Lejune, North Carolina. Someone transferred to a designated combat zone? The Morning Report would authorize the entry. Add Hostile Fire pay on line 17. Not taxable. Fifty-five dollars a month. Hell, I was getting it now, having just arrived to VietNam, a "newbee."

Then, it hit. The reality of Hostile Fire Pay, being in a war zone. Like "hot, molten rock" as D.H. Lawrence might put it, when that first Morning Report arrived listing a KIA (Killed in Action) who I knew, a guy I had trained with, a boy from Alabama; PFC William Earl Suttle of Prattville. Multiple shrapnel wounds. Nineteen years old. I didn't help wrap him in his poncho. I didn't lift his lifeless body onto a MedEvac chopper, nor remove it from the Huey trying in vain to keep the poncho from blowing off in the furious blast of the downdraft. Nor did I help place him along side the others; like stacks of cordwood in a row; no one there staring. No. I just read the Morning Report entry: KIA., multiple fragmentation wounds, Cam Lo. I made the proper notation on his pay record, trying, in vain, not to cry, remembering his soft Southern drawl, his love of the Crimson Tide, his joke about how Bear Bryant said he only recruited players who were "moBILE, aGILE and hosTILE," his good humor and laughter as he shouted "Roll Tide" while we trudged on the 50 mile Force March training at Camp Pendleton. Mobile. Agile. Hostile. Full battle gear training for VietNam. It was but a game then.

And now. Now I typed the entry on my manual Remington typewriter. Posted the SGLI (Servicemember's Group Life Insurance) payment of $10,000 to next-of-kin. Placed the thick yellow pay record in the worn pouch for transfer to Quang Tri then on to Headquarters Marine Corps, Washington, D.C. Hostile Fire pay terminated July 15, 1969, the day after my 21st birthday. No more birthdays for Suttle.

Yes, I had come a long way since learning to type in high school and dropping out of college. I didn't want to be drafted and my 2-S deferment was being revoked. So. I joined the Marine Corps. Weren't they supposed to be the toughest? Have the coolest uniforms? Off I went. No clue of the long history of military occupation in VietNam-the Chinese, the French, the Japanese, the Brits, and then the French again before us. Never heard of Dien Bien Phu. The Communists were trying to take over Asia, I was told, and we were there to stop them, to stop the dominoes from falling. If VietNam fell, then so would the surrounding states.

And, there I sat, at this funky fold out desk, that night in October of 1969, six miles from North VietNam, working feverishly after 12 hours of making endless entries, just the night after standing perimeter next to a 50 caliber machine gun, on top of a rat-infested bunker, hooked up to claymore mines on the wire, sleepless past my watch because I didn't trust the guy next to me to stay awake on his watch —- especially since he had smoked Pot, and, it was rumored, had drank typewriter fluid to get high...flashes of the rhythmic staccato from the .50 caliber shells bouncing off my helmet, the "bloop" of the M79 grenade launcher followed by the deafening explosion seconds later, my M16 jamming before the cease fire call came down the line...the sensation still with me. My introduction to hostile fire. The cacophony deafening. The chaos chilling. I longed for that dreaded typing class in Alaska where Mrs. Peterson would slap our knuckles with a ruler if we hit one more key after the bell rang on our timed exercises — no Nun at a Catholic school was harsher. I longed for hot water,. Hell, I longed for Potable water, unspoiled milk, real food, a comfortable bed. Safety. My mother's Chocolate Chip Cookies.

Then, this salty Staff Sergeant jumps from his seat, jungle boots in the air, eyes so unworldly wild, hitting the deck and covering his head. He had heard it coming. He was on his second tour, the first as a grunt at the Battle of Hue. I heard nothing. Nothing until it hit. "BROOOM!!"

A deafening explosion. Incoming! I had jumped to my feet, startled at the Staff Sergeant's sudden, unexpected dive. The rocket hit next to us, sending shrapnel through the hooch, the blast knocking me down. All I heard after that was a ringing. I felt warm moisture on my lips. Was I hit?! My nose was bleeding. A stinging on my cheeks. I quickly felt my core, my arms, my legs. All OK there.

Then I panicked. Couldn't find my M-16 in the smoke and confusion. Pulled my .45 pistol. We were on high alert, locked and loaded 24/7 because of recent enemy contact and firefights from Cam Lo to Dong Ha. I thought, Fuck Me!, they are coming through the wire! Then I thought, Jesus, the next round will be walked on top of us because our hooch was next to the motor pool and all our tanks. I called frantically to my friend Jake unaware that he couldn't hear anything either.

We low-crawled to what was left of the swinging door. I stopped at the door because I envisioned the NVA coming through the wire and picking us off like rats as we scrambled out. Another round hit nearby and Jake shouted "Fuck it!!" as he dove out. He screamed in pain. Was Jake hit?! Was he shot?! Hit by shrapnel?! FUCK IT!! I dove out and crawled to a ditch next to the putrid heads — 50 gallon barrels cut in half filled with shit. Jake was there, crouched low, holding a bloodied hand. He'd hit the concertina wire we had used with metal engineering stakes to secure the tin roof of our hooch after the last typhoon had blown it off. We had yet to remove the barbs. His hand was cut and bleeding profusely having hit the wire full stride. I wrapped it in a piece of my t-shirt.

We lay there for what seemed like an eternity. Waiting. Watching. Locked and loaded. Sweating. Silent. Unable to hear each other.

No more rockets. We crawled to what was left of the hooch and called out to the LT, to the Gunny, to the others. They had gone out the other side. No one was hit. Most had bloodied noses. All were shaken but grateful, some cursing at having to find and sort all the pay records scattered to hell and back.

Perhaps we had survived the blast because it wasn't a direct hit, or because the sandbags we had taken days to fill and stack around the hooch had taken much of the blast? We would not complain about filling sandbags again.

I took Jake to the Corpsman's aid station where they stitched him up, neither of us saying a word.

Hostile Fire Pay. Now, not just an entry on a pay record learned at Basic Dispersing School at Camp Lejune, North Carolina. The painful, visceral experience of what "hostile fire" meant seared upon my heart, my soul. Now, and forever, something carried; plaintive and haunting. Deeper than the deafening noises. And Subtle. Never again mobile. Never again agile. Forever hostile.

Almost
Jaime Lee Johnson

We had just gone through a residential area on patrol and were on our way back home, when I got the call over the radio for us to do a TCP near the CNN mosque. So instead of doing a right turn to go through checkpoint 1 and head back into the green zone, we passed it by and headed towards our objective.

Once there, we stopped our HMMVs in pattern and got out cones and concertina wire. But before we could even get anything set up, there was a concussive whump. We looked around to see where it came from and saw a smoke plume in the distance. It wasn't too far off and just as we all realized where it was, we heard several shots fired and the radio squawked calling for help. It was from checkpoint 1, where we were just about to go through not a few minutes ago.

We scramble to collect the wire and cones and decide to leave some behind, so we could just get going. Once at speed, we almost hit several cars before turning down that road, all of us expecting to see mayhem and bodies. But once there, it was just a few PSD SUVs and some contractors running about.

We set our vehicles in a defensive pattern and get out to assist. My squad leader asks one of the contractors what happened and is told an IED on the sidewalk to our right hit the lead vehicle.
After a few maneuvers and bounding tactics, we determine the area clear and decide how to get the downed SUV back to the FOB. After a few moments, we realized the contractors left and we had to break into the vehicle to get it out of gear, which failed. We just strapped a bunch of toe straps and literally dragged it home.

Making Monsters
Jim Marney-Petix

Boot camp was designed to give us the basic tools we needed to survive combat: effective use of weapons, high level of physical fitness, precise movement as part of a group, prompt response to orders, etc. Just as important, it was designed to change our mindset. We were taught to stop seeing human beings as people, the civilian mindset, and start seeing them as dangerous objects, the military mindset.

Of course, it had to be that way, or we wouldn't have been able to do our job. If we saw an enemy soldier as a frightened thirty-year-old with a wife and two kids who are trying to get into university so he can become a dentist, we'd never have been able to kill him. So a certain amount of demonizing had to take place; in Vietnam, the enemy became: gooks, slopes, slants, the yellow peril. It was all right to kill them because they were not exactly human.

Unfortunately, the enemy soldiers and the innocent civilians looked exactly the same. In fact, sometimes they were exactly the same. How is that possible? Children rigged up with explosives and sent to the G.I.'s to give them candy. Or a Vietnamese farm wife, carrying her market baskets on her shoulder, walking past a patrol on lunch break, counting her steps to give the local VC range and numbers information. Why would she do it? The Americans were foreigners who would be gone at the end of the year. The VC were locals who would be around for the next 20 years and knew where she lived. So everything was tension and paranoia, and we had a tendency to shoot anything that moved. I mean, they're *all* VC, right? Besides, they're just gooks.

Eventually, I learned enough about the locals to realize that the typical Vietnamese didn't know politics from his elbow. He was 100% behind whoever was holding the rifle. His goal was to live long enough to hold his grandchildren. His survival strategy was to be invisible. The business of his life was to keep his head down and grow his rice. And that didn't even count the old men, women, and children who were caught in the crossfire.

Unfortunately for me, I was raised to protect and nurture, and I began to question what I was doing. I even started seeing the NVA in a new light. There was no chance that they could be innocent civilians; they were uniformed enemy soldiers, but they were trying to drive out a foreign invader. That foreign invader was me. What was I doing there?

It wasn't long after I got out that the depression started, but it took a long time for me to figure out why. The iconic picture of the Vietnam War was a naked six-year-old girl running screaming down the road, trying to escape a napalm strike taking place behind her. That was what we were doing to the whole country, and I was part of it. I had become a monster.

Staying Alive
Bill Noyes

My heart is black. Ambush Patrol within my first week in country and I will walk point. American units have begun joint-ARVN patrols to show them the proper way. It is 1968 and someone decided they must begin to learn to do it right!

My black heart helps me melt easily into the night. No moon, no stars in the cloudy sky will light my way. My mind and body follow my thumping heart. Ghosts called to a séance, their quiet whispers beg caution. In my ears they screech fear, but without dread. I have trained for this night.

Our small squad leads their larger one toward the ambush position hidden within the tree line. The cloud covered paddies are full of water. The dike seems the only way to go as my foot feels the unseen path. Their following, sucking steps slide through the mud behind me. My ears reach past their noise as I step carefully forward.

My last step sinks quickly! Down I sink into bottomless liquid. Submerged into darkness I grip my rifle like a useless toy. Thrashing, the man behind me pulls me up and out; quiet soon returns.

Our leader decides to set up there, strung along the dike, and forgo the wood line. To proceed is risky since the enemy may have heard us coming. I had already shown the ARVN the important lesson about how to find the farmer's well. Thus, I spent a cold, wet night awaiting the enemy's un-humorous attack, as we waited in the open.

After training for about eight months, my first few weeks in country convinced me that I must focus with extraordinary effort on the details if I would survive in this unpredictable war. For a tired and over-burdened soldier this would not be easy; staying focused on issues that others might rather ignore. One must question every move to see clearly through the fog of war, as it is created in the mix of daily events with the deficiencies of others.

Others can too easily disregard important facets that are crucial to a danger that you must face. War provides almost a daily reoccurrence of this unfortunate truth. As soon as you notice a deficiency, no matter its size, seek its resolution. Disregarding it, to ignore its importance, is to welcome unexpected disaster. Most importantly, the ability to perceive future problems is obstructed by the smallest insensitivity that one will allow toward current choices that must be made.

As an example, I offer a tale about my first rifle which was issued just before going to join my infantry unit in the field. An old style M16 with three pronged suppressor at its muzzle, it was a deficient early model M16. They were all worn and already being replaced with a full suppressor version. The suppressor was not the problem and only identifies each model. It was not a weapon that was manufactured sufficiently ready for its first war.

I was presented the weapon at Dau Tieng Base the day I was sent to the field. No chance to test fire, just assurance that it was operable. I carried that rifle for at least two weeks on maneuvers without being allowed to test it. It was the rifle I carried when I stepped into the well within the first three days of my entrance to combat operations.

Finally, not being allowed to test fire my unknown weapon, with the help of an ARVN guard at a small outpost, I discovered that they had lied about the rifle. The guard, who carried an M-1 carbine, very much wanted to fire my black M16. Since he would avoid any negative reaction for his unauthorized shooting, I showed him how to set it on full automatic and gave it to him to try.

We expected a burst that would shatter the water near his target fifty yards away in the river. Only a single shot rang out! The casing had jammed before extraction. I cleared it and the second try produced the same result. The rifle's worn receiver was grabbing the expanded casing too tightly and the rifle's extractor was stripping instead of extracting the soft metal. The ARVN guard was very disappointed with the first M16 he'd tried to shoot!

I chose to carry an M60 machine gun for about a week before I finally got a new rifle. It was a lesson to me about other's lack of concern, their utter disinterest in an issue of vital importance to me. Small questions can yield big problems if left unattended.

I began to seriously question motives, my own and the motives of others, concerning actions I might take. This slowly led to my uncanny focus upon questions of what my enemy might be thinking, or might be hoping I would do. I began to consider a world of options based on a universe of possibilities, not merely my own needs and priorities regarding my next move. Men in battle are not there alone, in fact. Their contest represents far more than just their particular victory or defeat. It is a play far greater than those few actors on the stage, directed by an unseen master.

In my last day of battle, about eleven months after sinking into the well, a number of important decisions led to safety rather than death. It was a day of jungle patrolling, begun with improbable circumstances due to the vicissitude of war. After an early morning confrontation with the platoon staff, I was ordered to join a depleted squad to which I'd once belonged. Not happy with the situation, I grabbed a machine gun at the adopted squad location, thinking that at least I could avoid being assigned point-man duty with the gun. Machine guns are generally considered too important because of their heavy fire power to be put as a lead target for the enemy.

Our patrol began with the ARVN airborne company on the left, our American company on the right of the column, going into a jungle area of hidden enemy camps and storage locations. Soon, individual platoons were venturing in separate directions in search of bunkers and trails. This is a tactic to increase the chance for discovering hidden bunkers in heavy jungle. Our Third Platoon broke through the jungle chaos and found a slight trail leading through dense brush past an empty bunker. I found myself on point with my adoptive squad leader behind me. We were told to wait so that our lieutenant could search and report about the bunker that he had found.

We waited an inordinately long time while I surveilled the trail leading into the confining bushes to my front. While I could have moved a few feet forward to attempt to see around the next obstructive bush, something told me not to. As I looked at the bushes I worried what might lurk behind. I sensed my enemy's tension. Disaster awaited me on the other side of that bush. There seemed no alternative to the trail, except maybe busting through the thick thorns to the right.

I knew the enemy waited. I chose the sharp, two inch thorns on the right side obstructive bush. When the order came I moved off the trail toward the thorns. The fool behind me chose the trail but didn't wait for me to burst through on the right. It proved his last step in life as he moved past my old position on the trail.

The burst of automatic fire ignited an explosion of anger in me as I prepared to push through the thorns and confront the enemy. Then, I remembered that I could not trust the machine gun. It was maintained by a different squad from mine. I quelled my motivating anger and decided to lie down to test fire my gun, before advancing against the enemy not ten feet away. The event and the decisions came within a second, but as quickly, I knew I had been right to test the gun.

The gun's gas plug had not had its locking wire reinstalled. Consequently, the plug had shaken loose in the days and weeks of rattling inside the First Squad track. With the gas pressure reduced, the gun jammed each time it cycled. I tried it twice but the machine gun was now a single shot weapon! Had I attacked the bunker I now could see from the ground, I'd have had to work the action each shot to kill however many enemy I'd have found.

As I retreated through the thorns and branches behind me I saw the adopted squad leader laying in a pool of blood on the trail. I knew he was dead. He'd been blasted with the full burst from the bunker that was placed just beyond the thick bush obstructing the bend in the trail. I suspected at least two other enemy had joined in the long burst.

About twenty yards behind, the rest of the platoon had taken positions in bunkers and along the trail. They delivered an ineffective fire into the trees to their front. I directed their shooting more toward the bunker that I had seen. Then the platoon leader cried out that someone needed to retrieve the downed squad leader. There were no volunteers. But I agreed, so, I traded my inoperable machine gun for another squad mate's rifle and a bandolier of his magazines. He repaired the machine gun while I returned to the enemy bunker to fight and retrieve the body.

The first thing I did as I fell prone by the pool of blood was to fire the M16 at the bunker. I saw no breathing or movement by the squad leader, so suspected that he was beyond help. He was shot in the side and somewhere else and had spilled at least a gallon of blood to form the pool. I knew I could not fight for long with only the one bandolier but I had six or eight grenades in my pockets besides. I quickly threw four or five into and around the bunker. Two went off inside. In the bushes behind I shot and threw grenades. No one came up from the platoon until finally the medic came alone.

He checked the body and finally we struggled to begin moving the dead man back. As I guarded the front, the medic dragged the body almost half way by himself. The platoon continued their covering fire but no one came up to assault the bunker. Even after a gunship made a mini-gun run at the bunker that ended just in front of me, no attempted assault was made by the platoon. I decided to leave and returned to the platoon about twenty yards behind, leaving the squad leader's rifle lying at the threshold of the bunker entrance. It lay as a trophy for the men of the other side. Our platoon retreated to rejoin the company in a bombed clearing that was a safe distance from the enemy position. The enemy would be pummeled by heavy artillery and bombs.

We found our company along with the ARVN, filling the many craters there. We lay outside the filled craters while artillery and air strikes were delivered on to the enemy deeper in the jungle. Dirt clods and debris fell around us from each explosion. Another platoon had taken more casualties in a similar fight to ours. They had sustained more wounded but none killed. We would again patrol into the enemy positions after the artillery fire and bombing ended.

Soon, our companies rose and advanced again in a joint column, the ARVN Airborne on the left, the American B Company on the right. I had traded back the squad-mate's rifle and carried again the machine gun he had repaired. I believe that I was the last man, now, and I felt vulnerable to attack from both the side and behind.

We stopped and were told the ARVN would assault a position. We were to lay in support. I could see no one except the two or three men ahead in the thick jungle. Those men at first lay guarding to the side but soon were sitting up or even kneeling because of the humid heat near the ground as we waited. Their actual defense toward the side seemed more and more relaxed.

I lay looking down the barrel of my gun, picking the spot in nearby bushes where I guessed the enemy might first appear. My breathing was labored and I almost sat up but decided against it so to keep my low profile and a ready position. Then a trumpet blared, which was the ARVN signal to assault. We had no idea who it was since our unit used no trumpet signals. The firing immediately started and continued.

Bullets whizzed through the trees. They were enemy shots in response to the ARVN attack. I heard the loud clap of one bullet close to my ear, and immediately I knew that had I sat up instead of laying prone I might well have been killed. When the shooting stopped we got ready to move. Maybe due to casualties or reorganization, the Americans started moving past the ARVN along a trail and away from the area.

As we passed some ARVN I could view the result of their attack. The dead man would not be taken out by helicopter but carried by his comrades. I knew that I had nearly gone, several times that day, to wherever dead soldiers will meet, but for a few timely and seemingly unimportant decisions. Bullets cannot be dodged, but their effects are the result of important choices one must make, perhaps at inopportune times while at war.

War presents unavoidable threat to the soldier. However, after the threat of battle there are still many lingering threats to the average soldier. Merely returning home from a war is no assurance that a threat to safety will not develop. Chaos and confusion is not just a condition of the battlefield for the human mind but will linger in real and important ways long after battle. Battle is also a psychic and spiritual affair, and there is no avoidance possible in its aftermath in these realms.

In the middle of my tour I'd captured a Chicom pistol from a corpse we had killed almost a month before. He had bled and rotted all over the gun. I cleaned it, registered it and took it home as a war trophy, along with the six rounds still in its magazine. It was the only such trophy acquired in my company, so far as I knew, and it always carried a vile smell thereafter.

Returned from the war, I immediately re-entered the college I had attended before I'd been drafted. The transition from battle to civil life was challenging and it was an emotional shock for which I was unprepared. In truth, the Military, the Veterans Administration, along with the society around me at that time, were equally unprepared and unready, for various reasons, to deal with the aftermath of war.

I slept for days from exhaustion. I dreamed the same confounding dreams each night about the various battle situations I had encountered. The same people always died, no matter what the ridiculous scenario would be. There was no easy relief from re-living the experiences I had had. As well, my movements and reactions seemed outside my control each day. I moved in a world apart, no matter where or who I was near. I sought only to get through each day, and avoid any more challenge than I seemed destined to endure.

Within a few months I felt spent, and very confused by my

predicament. No change seemed possible and in a fit of self-pity I had the war trophy I had taken loaded and pointed at my head. Death presents no fear for the soldier, it being just the expected outcome of living. Within a moment I would not have to think about it anymore!

Solutions are never as easy in life, as are problems to be had. Don't expect a solution so much as fully appreciate your problems, in order to make the most of adverse circumstances. This perspective will allow, at least, for active change. Spiritual growth can happen during adversity but must be active, and sought, for it is never awarded otherwise.

Anger, that the enemy bullet would find its target so far from the battlefield, was what stopped my finger. I saw the corpse's lipless smile in a flash, the man who'd had the gun, as I lowered the gun and then un-cocked the hammer. I needn't stop the anger this time, as I had done during my last battle. Righteous and useful anger is helpful, and should be sustained. It can take us in the direction we want to go.

Anger can at times sustain life but spirit requires the willfulness of understanding and the control of self, not force, to go to another level in life. Understanding this, there is no easy trick to be learned to overcome the negative effect military service can have on one's mind and spirit. Fear and anger can force immediate action, which is needed while under threat, but usually not the correct decisions required to sustain spiritual and emotional wellbeing after war.

Stay focused on your problems (at war) and see it for how it might benefit you, not how others dictate you should see it. This will allow options you otherwise might miss, and connect your perceptions to realities beyond yourself. Then you may well discover talents previously unappreciated, and develop facility and appreciation for your situation, no matter how vexing, during your time at war.

First Blood, October 1968

Bill Noyes

A leg left connected by a mere strand of tissue was my introduction to the war. I was new to the field, so the fire support base was the second and largest of the mud-filled camps I entered in the early days of my tour. Its name is unremembered, if ever known and I would quickly leave it, anyway.

The leg was someone else's. He had stood near a burn barrel that exploded when lit. Boom! A shard from the barrel had nearly severed his leg near the sand-bagged wall where I sat. I was the first to reach his side.

He screamed and then cried, as he gripped my left hand and would not let go. My right attempted to hold the leg close to its body so the strand of flesh would not break. My squad mate, Hollins, was second there, to console the Brother and hold his head.

Medics quickly arrived and the man with his nearly detached leg was soon taken away. He was flown to a base camp, and we heard nothing more, except rumors. Maybe he was an engineer, not infantry. No one knew his name, or how the grenade or explosive had been put in the barrel. We worried that it was not mistaken but placed by a VC. There was little any of us could do but attend to the wounded, prepare for the next time, and hope we each would survive.

CHAPTER II
Handrails

"There is no instance of a nation benefitting from prolonged warfare."
—Sun Tzu's "The Art of War"

Handrails are used on ships to assist sailors to climb stairs. Ship ladders are steep and almost impossible to climb without the assistance of those handrails. A sailor in our group of writers described how important these handrails are in everyday life onboard a ship. It's like one of those critical elements of everyday life that we take for granted.

The discussion eventually turned to the handrails in our lives, those unseen assists we use daily and can't do without. This chapter deals with the assists that were used to guide us through our lives regarding PTSD and trauma.

In this context, handrails represent the transition from trauma to healing. The form of these handrails is as varied as the trauma itself. In this chapter, the veteran's handrails include recalling specific events, identifying life before the trauma, recognizing something wrong, deciding to take action, failed attempts, and physical experiences. However, each person has their own handrails and uses them in the most appropriate way for them.

The reader is encouraged to identify the handrails they have found helpful in dealing with trauma. If no handrails have been identified, start looking for them. They are there.

Recovery
G. Craige Edgerton

Time can be your friend,
Or your hidden fiendish enemy.
Memories return, some as if yesterday,
Lost in a life well lived.
While others emerge, hidden away for years,
Causing a life of turmoil
Wallowing in those yesterday memories.

Those destructive memories
Can dissipate only when spoken.
But there has to be a listening.
For us, fellow vets
Are the listeners.
Recovery begins in the
Speaking out loud
Of those memories
Buried so long, so deep.

Speak up, O Brothers!
Yank the thorn out.
Tell your story for
Your story is my story,
Is his story, is their story,
Is all of our stories.

Recover the memories
And let them go.
Release them into
An accepting space

Held by your Brothers,
And accept the Healing.

Depression
Jim Marney-Petix

I was working in Redwood City on Seaport Blvd. and living in north Fremont near Mission and Niles Canyon Rd. My second wife and I were still together. So, it must have been the early to mid-90s, and I was suicidal. There was no other way to put it. I was in so much pain I would have done anything to stop it. And I was convinced that it would be like this forever. I had a plan worked out in considerable detail. It was a good plan; I was proud of it. So why am I still alive? I was too depressed to carry out the plan. Getting the details lined up takes work; I just didn't have it.

I had been depressed before the 90s, but that was the worst. I got some halfway-decent meds, and I started feeling better. The suicide went away, but the depression never did. Once or twice a year, I wouldn't be able to get out of bed for a week at a time. At least three times, I lost a job because my struggles with depression affected my performance. During most of this time, I was a test engineer. I came up with a couple of brilliant ideas, but I could never rise above mid-level because I was dealing with panic attacks and depression and could not follow them up. A few years before retirement age, I became a schoolteacher in a local district. I came up with a couple of innovations for teaching science and started an after-school science club, but I was asked to retire before I wanted to because my depression interfered with my prepping for class.

My depression continues to plague me to this day. My church lost its treasurer, and I was asked to step in. A church treasurer has a thousand things to keep track of, but none of them are rocket science. It should be no big deal. But when I sit there looking at the things that have to be done, I just can't make sense of them. Then I'll have a panic attack and have to get away from them. That will lead to feelings of worthlessness and despair.

I Was Her Son
Jaime Lee Johnson

Bags packed and on the road. I feel excited and extremely sad. I'm on a one-way trip from what was my home for the last 3 years. The men I've known and served with now behind me. I now take steps forward to return to a life that was before my life as a soldier.

I'm in line for the TSA guard to check my ID and send me through the x-ray machine. I'm nervous about scuffing my class A's that I'm wearing due to not wanting them crushed in the belly of the plane. I shuffle forward, placing my CamelBak in the bin, followed by my freshly polished patent leather shoes and discharge packet materials. I take off my class A jacket and just before it follows the shoes, a TSA agent tells me I can hold it in the scanner before going myself. I thank him for the consideration and I carry on my way to my flight's gate.

I'm at a bar drinking a soda and picking at some fries as I watch a football game. The anxiety of my travels still rushes through me. My flight is called and as I go to pay, the bartender tells me my money is no good there and that I should get to my flight. I try to force the issue, but he was having none of it. I thank him and move to the gate.

On the plane and taking small steps to my seat. Hoping to have a window seat so I can sleep off my slightly trembling nerves. I discover I have an isle seat and think "Just my luck!" due to having my A's on. I'm barely seated when a lovely woman in the isle informs me there is a first-class seat for me. I first think it's a stewardess misunderstanding my seat arrangement, but it's just another passenger. I tell her I'm in the right seat, hoping to not delay the flight. She tells me it's her seat and is requesting a swap. I reluctantly agree, retrieve my gear, and follow my escort to first-class.

As my mind races to understand what's happening, she tells me her son served in the Marines, was killed in Afghanistan, and that she felt obligated to thank one of his brothers. I'm almost floored with emotion and struggle to hold back a tear when we're suddenly in, from what I consider, a whole new plane after entering the first class section.

She guides me to my new seat and, respectfully, asks me for a hug. We embrace and just as I let her go, she says, "Welcome home, son." I barely hold it together until she leaves, then I practically collapse into the soft leather seat. The tears I held back earlier came crashing through like a tidal wave. The feelings I've had for the last 5 hours overwhelm me to the point of bursting through my chest. Loss, grief, anger, resentment, and a sense of duty stream down my face as the plane takes me home.

The Door
Sunny "Dos" Dosanjh

It is a small miracle that I am actually here
Death came knocking on my door
And luckily, I could not hear it

The mind is lost
The body is heavy
My soul is out of reach

Existence has lost its meaning
Beauty has lost its allure
Love…maybe that who is knocking on my door

Pain and suffering have become normal
Sadness and despair tag along also
I lie at the bottom, in complete darkness

The desire for happiness is gone
Joy and love are just words, empty
My spirit is broken

If there is a way forward
I know not of it
In darkness is each step taken

I am rudderless and directionless
I have no clue where I'm heading
And my journey is completely alone

My melancholy is visible

My face is frozen in time
I do not remember who I am

The knock on the door is louder now
I wonder if it is Death or Love
I open the door.

The Mirage
Sunny "Dos" Dosanjh

And there it was
Hope Eternal

It appeared
Seemingly out of nowhere

And that's exactly where I was
Nowhere

But now I had a vision
Of somewhere

Somewhere where the birds sing
And flowers bloom

Somewhere where the best of humanity
Is on display

I wonder if it's real
Or a mirage

So I take a step forward
Into the mystic

Hero's Journey
G. Craige Edgerton

The scrub savannah of South Texas
My home, home on the range.
Remote and isolated
Miles from any significance.
An ordinary world for ordinary folks.

The beckoning was always there.
There's got to be more than this.
Reading transported me to unknown worlds,
Just itching to be explored.
They call me, and I resist.
But only for a while.

Do I seek treasure or danger? Or both?
I fantasize being a Marine
With rifles fashioned from mesquite branches
And big-eared jack rabbits for target
As I deploy and maneuver in my home,
The Wild Horse Desert.

Dress blues capture my fancy
Before my third college year.
My chance to fulfill a dream.
Lingering in my unconscious are
Those same Mesquite branches
And big-eared rabbits of my youth.

I accept the call
Becoming Second Lieutenant, USMC.

Proud, upright, oozing patriotism,
My mission: Save the world
From ominous dominos
Destined for our sacred shores.

My talisman for this hallowed journey?
The rich history of Marine Corps lore
Deeply embedded in carefully
Orchestrated stories
Or possibly meticulously contrived propaganda.

I accept the test, pass the training,
And board the transport to a curious land
With unintelligible language and
Pajamas and conical straw hats, the
Practical, nay fashionable, haute couture.

My credulity is tested as I fire 105 MM howitzers
Streaking through blanketed stars
Into inky skies in search of unknowable targets.
"Harassing and Interdicting" is their moniker.
Big-eared rabbits are clearly absent.

The cannon fire landed,
I know not where.
A sanitized killing,
Never seeing "Charlie"
Face to face.

I did my job; I passed the test.
Never questioning.
"Yes sir,"; "right away sir,"; "as you say, sir."
I was a good Marine, challenged over and over.
Obediently following obtuse orders.

.

Promoted in the field to First lieutenant.

But the wounds linger.
The body is sound.
The psyche, not so much.
Moral injury an unknown term, newly learned
Lived with every day
Some 50 years later.

But this journey is not a hero's.
No parade, plaques, kudos or bands.
No reward to place on the mantle.
No hat spewing "Look at me".
Just a forgotten Marine
Hiding his disillusioned journey.

The journey seemingly ends,
I am intact, back to family, normalcy.
The ordinary world for ordinary folks.
My safe place, where I began.

The moral injury is later revealed,
Hidden deep in the recesses of my soul.
The true hero's journey concludes,
Facing the demons, learning from them.
Those monsters my ultimate teachers.

Captain Casey
Doug Nelson

We listened to the enemy's communications. And one of his comrades on a hill aimed a mortar round in our direction that took you away from us. But for a breath of breeze, it would have missed you and hit one of us, or hit no one at all.

I was sent to get an ambulance for you. I didn't know what one looked like, so I came back without finding one. They told me you didn't make it.

Later, back home, I tried to tell my folks about you. About when my newfound buddies said, "It's time to meet the captain." I saw dirt fly up out of the hole you were helping dig before I saw you. You said, "I won't have you guys do anything I wouldn't do." You were very patient when I had a hard time learning my job. And those are the last words I heard you speak was to yell at us to get into the bunker you helped us build.

Chris, you were traveling in a truck company, returning to us, when you stepped on a mine in the roadway. Our dog, Lady, waited for your return for weeks afterward.

Kindness for Mom and Dad was to say, "Wrong place at the wrong time." Or, "Glad it wasn't you." It only made me feel worse that it was both of you.

Captain, Christopher, we were young, and none of us knew how to grieve for you. We never talked about having lost you, just kept it all inside. Weeks later when the chaplain, who didn't know you or any of us, said a prayer, all of our eyes rested on your helmets, stuck on upright rifles, bayonets in the ground. By then, the defensive numbness had set in and would last decades.

I had to see your names thirty years later on the Wall we built for ourselves in Washington before the tears would run down my cheeks. In those days, I worked near the wall. Before I would move away, I walked over to see your names one last time and to lay one last salute on you. I said my goodbyes, but you rode to California with me in the back seat of my mind. I wasn't leaving you. I should have known I could not have.

Are there different sorts of grieving to lament the role of chance or the role of the indifferent whims of those in power, either of which takes a brother from us?

The farmer prays for his field of hay, while the vintner down the road prays for dryness for his grapes; neither wanting to take a chance on the chance, they petition their old, white Male being.

My mom believed in God but also prayed with my dad in the night, begging please don't let anything happen to my little boy. Captain Casey, Chris, you had a mom and dad, too.

All too often, my friends, we are in the range of mortar or rocket fire. Our helicopter goes down, our truck rolls over some improvised mine, or someone makes a mistake with a weapon.

And all the while, old white men who never went to war pray for the annihilation of our enemies, the destruction of their crops, and the suffering of their children at their Prayer Breakfast.

And you and I, every boy and girl destined for Iraq and Afghanistan, are, from the instant we sign on the dotted line and raise our right hand, are at their mercy, or lack of it.

I would have done anything for you, Captain. But I didn't know what.

Veteran's Day Parade
G. Craige Edgerton

As I strolled alongside my fellow veterans down First Street, the crowd waved flags and cheered from the densely packed sidewalk to my right and left. Adulation rang out in the cool, crisp fall air. But to my ears, the sounds were strangely muted. I saw mouths opening and closing but couldn't hear what they said. My head felt like it was wrapped in a dense fog that dulled my mind, unlike the life-giving mist that often enfolded the Santa Cruz mountains just a few miles west. As I walked amidst the floats and festivities, I felt like a disoriented tourist lost in a new city. And yet, despite my mental haze, I reveled in the clear blue November sky, the weather that made him glad he left Texas so many years ago.

"This could be a terrific theme for a Twilight Zone episode," he thought as discomfort welled up in him.

Looking back, he could see the local Kiwanis float with many older veterans, mostly from the Vietnam War, sitting on chairs, smiling and waving, with their wives there for support. The local Kiwanis President led the charge out front, proudly waving a large American flag. Although he was also a Vietnam veteran, there was no way I would be found sitting on that float.

Walking in the Veterans Day parade, surrounded by raucous South Bay patriots, I struggled for mental clarity. *Do they have any idea what they are cheering for? Do they understand that war is not something to be saluting? Do they understand what true patriotism really is? They are like I was when I graduated from college in my dress whites, patriotic, and idealistic.* Thoughts and memories of Vietnam ricocheted in my mind but couldn't quite surface. The resistance was just too strong.

As my internal battles raged, booming music from the high

school band ahead of me seemed like an attack from the outside; each beat felt like a *thump* on my head. I wanted to leave the parade, but unfortunately, I was stuck. My friend Dave had been kind enough to accompany me, proudly wearing his Marine Corps Corporal uniform from nearly six decades ago. The jacket and pants still fit him, as he had remained in remarkably good shape for a man in his 80s. Dave, eight years my senior, was genuinely gratified to be there, soaking up the crowd's cheers. I was in regular street clothes. After my discharge, I'd thrown my Marine Corps uniform into a trash bin in June 1971. I wanted nothing more to do with that uniform after my service had ended.

I did not want to be here. I was "encouraged" to do so because my PTSD therapist from the Vet Center said it would do me good.

"Just try it," the counselor had said. "You might find that the support and acknowledgment of an unknown, admiring public is a breakthrough in your being pissed off at the Marine Corps and the Johnson administration. You don't have to do it again if it doesn't work out for you."

So, against my better judgment, I was walking in the 2018 Veteran's Day Parade in San Jose, California.

Farewell
Sunny "Dos" Dosanjh

From where came that Love
Did I know what stirred my soul
I do not have the words
But I will open my heart to you

Love pulls me in
Draws me close
It's useless to ignore
It's hopeless to resist

So, I pack my bags and depart
To that calling from afar
Love is in my heart
I hope you know what that means

Why Vietnam?
Jim Marney-Petix

Do you remember that movie? President Johnson narrated it. As I remember, the gist of his message was that we were trying to keep a big guy, The North, from beating up a little guy, The South. For my twenty-year-old self, it was a good enough pep talk. Still, when I got a little older and started thinking in terms of economic self-interest, vital resources, strategic location, etc., it made a lot less sense because Vietnam didn't have any of those things. With no air force or navy, it wasn't even close to a military threat. So why? To give it back to the French?

Oh, yeah, the domino effect. The notion that if we allowed the other countries of the world to fall to Communism, then we would be fighting a massive monolithic enemy at some point in the future. The implication being that the rest of the world would be the Soviet Union on steroids, and the US would be the sole remaining holdout. Scary enough, I admit.

The trouble was that domino doctrine discounted the fact that cultures that have hated each other for 4,000 years don't automatically become blood brothers because they're now both communist. The first thing the communist regime in Vietnam did after unifying the country was go to war with their communist neighbors.

By indulging a "Communism is cancer!" hysteria, we dropped ourselves into an unwinnable war. The NVA had a sanctuary in the north that we could not invade out of fear of an overreaction by China, so there was no way to corner them. They had a route for moving troops and supplies to the south that we could not block, so there was no way to starve them out. And they were never going to give up the fight no matter how long it took, so there was no way to outlast them. Eventually, the war became so expensive that we could no longer sustain it. So, for no clear political, economic, or national security advantage, we left 54,000 twenty-year-olds on the battlefield and lost even more than that at home to suicide and substance abuse. Thanks a lot, Assholes.

We Went
G. Craige Edgerton

We went. Most willingly. Some not.
But we went.
For adventure, for discipline
In memory of our forefathers,
For duty. For some,
Uncle Sam cajoled us.

But we went.

And we came home,
Full of pride, we served well.
Others, wounded of body and mind.
Lost and confused.
Many in body bags.

No bands or parades.
No "thank you" or "welcome home".
Just seeking normalcy. Wife, 2 kids,
An adequate job, no trip wires.
Fading back into society.
Invisible we were,
Soldiers or Marines.
Trying to forget.

But we went.
And most came home.

Falling Apart
Sunny "Dos" Dosanjh

"*The loneliest moment in someone's life is when they are watching their whole world fall apart and all they can do is stare blankly.*" F. Scott Fitzgerald, The Great Gatsby.

There is nothing you can do but stare. It's like watching a movie, but you're the main character. Everything is crumbling and falling apart.

Job gone
Money gone
Home gone
Wife gone
Kids gone
All my life's memorabilia…gone
Even sanity has left.

You stare, and there is nothing left in your mind to fill the blank void of "no" thoughts. There is no one you can turn to…who would or could even fathom what is transpiring.

That's the moment you find yourself…alone.

Even well-wishers like parents or siblings have no idea of the magnitude of loss, grief, pain, angst, misery, desperation, depression, anxiety, terror, nightmares, catastrophes and suicidal thoughts that are unraveling.

There are no good luck charms, positive affirmations or divine intervention that stops not just one thing…but everything…your whole world just falls apart.

Had I not just experienced it to this depth…I would have said the obvious phrases like "this too shall pass" or look on the bright side, or "you have your health" There are no words, nor phrases that even begin to address the sheer magnitude of the fall. You are at deaths' door and thus the blank stare. Shocked into numbness.

In the darkness you lie.

In the darkness you try to think or feel you way forward…but it's all in vain

In the darkness, you have been check-mated…game over.

It has and continues to be the loneliest moments of my life watching 40 years of toiling, scratching, clawing to shape out an existence and watch it all, everything collapse like a deck of cards.

Thus, I know that stare. It's worse than death because you're alive to see it all break down. Everyone and everything departs, even Love.

So here I sit and all I can do is stare blankly.

Memorial

Nick Butterfield

Be-yond clouds
Simply a dash (-)
Between two numbers

A birth-
A death

Where be-tween is no
longer a verb

No ranks
No steps
No hope

Just the privilege
and sweetness
of grief

Fri 24 Nov 19
Jim Marney-Petix

0355: I'm awake. Sometimes it's because of dreams so painful that I have to escape. Sometimes, it's a sense of danger. This morning, I don't know why, I just know I'm awake.

It has happened often enough that I know if I just lie here and try to get back to sleep, I never will. I don't want to wake up my wife, so I go to the living room and use the recliner. I keep a blanket rolled up beside the chair for mornings like this. Sometimes, I can get back to sleep for a couple more hours, and sometimes, I can't.

If I can't get back to sleep after about half an hour, I will start reading. The problem is that I will read compulsively for the rest of the day. I shouldn't complain; it's a lot better than drinking all day, but it's just as time-consuming.

0700: My wife is up, so I can start moving about with a clear conscience. I go into the bathroom and do the usual stuff, but at 0900, when she calls me for breakfast, I'm still not dressed. I've been reading. So, I go to breakfast in my bathrobe.

0900: We eat breakfast and plan our day. Our agreement is that she cooks, and I clean up. I head back to the bathroom to finish getting dressed, and then I start reading.

1030: I'm dressed and ready to start the clean-up. It's no big deal: put the perishables in the fridge, empty the dishwasher, put the clean dishes away, start refilling the dishwasher for tonight's load, hand wash the few items that need it, wipe down the counters and stove. Twenty minutes to a half hour, right?

I'm facing the dirty dishes and having an anxiety attack. I start reading to calm down. It runs to half an hour. I open the dishwasher and empty it. It takes about fifteen minutes. I start reading again. Another half hour and I load the empty dishwasher. I start reading again. There are a few things that have to be washed by hand. I start reading again.

1230: I decide to do a laundry. I drag the clothes basket out to the garage. I lean against the car and start reading. At last, the washer is loaded and the laundry started. I start reading until time to load the dryer.

1350: Start the dryer and set the timer. Start reading.

1450: I'm still reading when the timer alarm sounds and having trouble stopping. My wife doesn't like clothes to remain in the dryer too long because she believes they will wrinkle. So when I get out to the garage, I find my wife emptying the dryer. I'm feeling judged, and I lose my temper. I think I have frightened her because she backs away. I finish unloading the dryer and start feeling guilty. I start folding clothes with her by way of apology. It doesn't help.

1730: Supper. Clean up follows the same pattern as this morning's clean up. I do a little bit of cleaning and a lot of reading. I start the dishwasher so anything she needs for tomorrow's meals will be clean.

1930: I sit down at the desktop and attempt to write. I start reading the news stories and I can't stop. I don't get any writing done.

2035: My wife is going to bed. I still can't stop reading the news stories. It's a little ridiculous actually. I'll scan the whole news page looking for stories that interest me. When I have read them all, I refresh the news page looking for new stories. Then I'll do it again, and then again. Some nights I will do that for hours.

2120: I give up on trying to write. I pour eight ounces of red wine and settle down with a DVD. It is a collection of half-hour lectures on astronomy, so I can stop anywhere and come back to it later without losing anything.

2210: Eight more ounces of wine.

2305: Eight more ounces of wine and about ten ounces of plain yogurt.

2345: I'm falling asleep on the couch. I close down and go to bed.

0410: I'm awake.

Getting To Sleep
Jim Marney-Petix

A young woman, obviously pregnant, with three bullet holes in her chest and abdomen, one of which probably killed her baby. An old man lying face down with the left side of his face and neck blown away. Two NVA soldiers lying on a field LZ waiting for pick up until maggots are coming out of their eyes and mouth. One had a picture of a woman about his age, possibly his wife, and a GI shredded by a hand grenade at close range. A ten-year-old boy was caught in the blast, too. A box, a little bigger than a shoe box, usually made of wood, wrapped in a grey ribbon, containing ashes. Fire and screams. Explosions and screams. This is what waits for me at night and sometimes during the day.

For decades, it has taken about six standard drinks to get to sleep. That's a six-pack of beer, or a half-pint of brandy, or a bottle of wine essentially every night for over forty years. I do my drinking between 10:00 at night and 2:00 in the morning, so, so far, it hasn't bled into my daytime activities, but I know it's not good for me. Besides the damage to my body, there's the disruption of my sleep cycles.

When I finally got up the courage to tell my doctor, he put me on Trazodone because it "Won't disrupt my normal sleep cycle." Unfortunately, for me, 'not disrupting' means letting me dream, and dreaming wakes me up—disrupting my sleep cycle. Also, one pill makes me drowsy, but it doesn't put me to sleep. If I take more than one, I get to sleep, but I end up with a major drug hangover the next day. So, I'm back on the booze: it knocks me out, I don't dream, and I get less hangover. My current favorite is red wine.

Kids At Play
Jaime Lee Johnson

On patrol again. This time, through a few neighborhoods. At first, they look how one would expect them to look. Mismatched walls, abandoned cars, spaghettified power lines, trash everywhere. Our HMMWV barely made it through the alley, but we it did and we turned a corner. I was suddenly in a different world. Kids at play wearing clean clothes, well kept yards, matching homes, the cars seemed to be in regular use, and not a scrap of trash in sight. We move on to our next patrol point.

We arrive at the local (what we considered) strip mall and put up a temporary check point. I'm ordered to get into the turret, so the others can get out and place the cones and wire, while I keep an ear on the radio. As I visually scan the locals with the radio mic in hand, I see 2 children playing. One is searching for something, while the other, a little girl, just sits in the street. A street covered in pot holes the cars passing by desperately try to avoid. In the process, they almost hit the girl … but always seem to miss her. The alley is filled with trash and debris.

I look back at the little girl. She is absolutely filthy and wearing what could only be described as rags. There came a moment when our eyes meet and I wave. She waves back, but with the look of deep loss and despair I hadn't seen before or since.

For years after coming home, I would see her in a nightmare involving an IED. I would wake in the middle of the night, covered in sweat.

Huckeropter
Doug Nelson

I was only a toy, made in China of red plastic
with yellow rotor blades like the real ones
to fit a little boy's dream
of machines that flew overhead
that made pup pup pup pup pup noises.

His daddy gave me to him
because he ran outside to see every one
that flew over.
My little boy did his best to fit what he heard
with what he was able to say,
hence "huckeropter".

The boy carried me around the house,
as fast as his little feet would take him
raising me up above his head
calling out pup pup pup pup pup.

The boy grew, played soccer,
learned to play guitar well enough,
and found a girl he liked.
Some years after my last flight,
his dad found me in the garden,
a blade broken off, buried in dirt,
and I went the way of Christmas trees,
popsicle sticks, and plastic army men.

And the boy, who's a dad, and his dad
remember me by what remains,
my name,
"huckeropter".

Reparations
Nick Butterfield

Could this place transcend time
when now has won.
This plane seems to be going fast
through the night and turbulence.
Enough so when we land we could
fix this thing.
With eyes shut wide open could once
again see
and someday fix this thing
that once was broken.

Coming Home
G. Craige Edgerton

I left Vietnam as part of the Marine Corps' initial withdrawal on November 8, 1969, even though it took another 5 ½ years for the war to officially end. I departed from Da Nang on a Navy ship, the same location I had arrived 7 months earlier, and, after 12 days at sea, landed at Camp Hansen on Okinawa. Camp Hansen had been active since WWII's Battle of Okinawa.

I was assigned to be an S-2 intelligence officer even though I had absolutely no training in intelligence and no idea what to do. Eventually, I discovered that intelligence meant gathering information, usually on threats to the unit or other U.S. interests. What the hell the Marine Corps needed to gather intelligence in a peaceful place like Okinawa was beyond me. Were the locals going to invade a fully armed Marine Corps base with experienced combat troops? Were there evil terrorists lurking nearby? I never unearthed any intelligence useful to the Marines except to note that servicemen should be careful in Kim City, the bar-laden local village across from the base entrance, which was crawling with prostitutes, thugs, and other nefarious locals.

Luckily, I had a gunnery sergeant (gunny) who was an intelligence specialist, so I let him do all the important work. As an intelligence officer, the most intelligent thing I did was to let the gunny take charge! This lesson would serve me well in later life.

I had been on Okinawa only a couple of weeks when the gunny called me aside one morning and said, "Lieutenant, you're going home. Go see the Captain for your orders. You leave tomorrow morning on a C-130 transport. We got a notice from the Red Cross that your mom is extremely sick. When the Red Cross calls, you go home". *Huh? My mom is sick? This must be serious to send me home on such short notice,"* I thought. The next few days were a blur as I returned to Abilene, Texas, where I met my dad at the airport and got the latest news about my mom. She was being treated at the Baylor Scott and White Hospital in Belton, Texas, in the final stages of cancer.

"Really? When did you know she was dying from cancer?" I asked my dad incredulously.

"I've known for a few weeks," he replied.

I didn't know before I left for Vietnam that cancer had been suspected in my mom. She didn't want to worry me. As her health gradually deteriorated, my dad chose not to tell any of the family until the very end. My mind flashed back to the last time I saw my mom, about 8 months earlier, at that very same airport on my way to Vietnam.

The next morning, at my dad's suggestion, I put on my dress blues, stored at the family home in Abilene, and the two of us drove to the hospital in Belton.

All I remember about that day was walking into the hospital room and seeing my mom in bed, her eyes closed. The nurse gently woke her. Slowly, she opened her eyes and struggled to focus. She was conscious enough to recognize me, but just barely. After what seemed like an interminable time, although it was only seconds, a slow smile came over her face; she was glad to see her son back from the war, safe and sound. Though she could not talk, I hugged her, and we exchanged loving gazes. I remained until she fell back into unconsciousness due to her morphine sedation.

My dad and I returned to Abilene with plans to meet a medical air ambulance at the airport the next morning, as my mom had wanted to die peacefully at home. Unfortunately, she died on the flight back home in the care of my grandmother, Edna, a nurse who had come to be with her daughter in her last hours. My mom was buried on a cold, windy, overcast November day at Elmwood Memorial Park in Abilene, Texas. Dressed in my formal Marine Corps dress blue uniform, I greeted long-time family friends as best I could. My brothers and sister had also been kept in the dark by Dad as to how bad my mom's condition was, and they were still in shock as, like me, they had no idea her death was so imminent. Some of them were torn between being furious with Dad and the sadness of their mom's death. As the service concluded and the attendees departed, I looked back at the empty grave site and returned by myself for one last goodbye.

After the funeral, the family gathered at home. A friend of my dad approached me to express his condolences. He asked if I had been to Vietnam.

"Yes, sir, I just returned from there," I replied.

"Tell me," the man asked, "What kind of an island is Vietnam?"

Huh, what did he just ask? I thought, my mind swirling. *What kind of an island? Are you out of your freaking mind?*

"I'm sorry, sir, but Vietnam is not an island but part of mainland Southeast Asia," I politely replied.

I wanted to say, *You stupid shithead, American men are dying over there every day, and you don't even take the effort to know it is part of mainland Asia and not an island?* But I bit my tongue and remained polite, even as anger and incredulity raged inside. *If folks here in the good old US of A don't care enough to know the basic geography of Vietnam, why was I risking everything to go there?* Looking back, I wondered how a seemingly innocent conversation could stick with me for over 50 years. That man and the words he spoke are still as vivid as if the conversation had occurred this morning.

Was this the moment I stopped being a proud Marine, where I started to seriously question what I had done in Vietnam? The staying power of this memory told me that something had changed in me at that moment and that my perspective on the world would never be quite the same again.

A few days after the funeral, I received orders to report to Albany, Georgia. It would be my final stint in the Marine Corps. I was assigned to be the company commander for about 40 Marines who, like me, couldn't wait to get out. I had seen the attitude of the "lifers," those who committed 25 to 30 years in the Marine Corps, and

I wanted nothing to do with that lifestyle. Even though the Marine Corps Supply Depot at Albany was considered the "country club" of the Marine Corps, the lifestyle of being a Marine, the blind obedience to orders, the saluting, the inherent false superiority of officers, the ultimate mission of killing as many people as efficiently as possible, the lack of entrepreneurship, the rigidity of rules that often made no sense to me, all of these choices, not only didn't fit my lifestyle and belief system but were repugnant to me. My service end date of June 1, 1971, couldn't come fast enough!

My company sergeant was scheduled to retire soon, the same month I was to be discharged, so the two of us made a pact. If the sergeant took care of my duties until then, I would give him the highest final recommendation so the sergeant could secure maximum pay upon retirement. This gave me the freedom to feel almost like a civilian in my final months.

As a result of that pact and the freedom it allowed me, on October 10th, 1970, eight months before escaping the Marines, I married the woman with whom I had the three-day party in San Francisco before I deployed, a year and a half earlier. We lived in Albany, GA, until I was discharged. We eventually moved to Austin, TX, and finally to San Jose, CA, where we settled, started a business, and raised our family.

Looking at the end of my Marine Corps service, I was embarrassed and regretful. Remembering my 10-year-old self, who proudly carried my stick rifles through the Texas coastal savannah, I was overcome with disappointment. When I finally received my discharge from the Marines, I was adamant that I would never reveal to anyone, except my wife, immediate family, and close friends, that I had served. Months before, I had decided to bury this part of my life and get back on track, starting from where I left off before the war as a new college graduate.

War Sucks

Nick Butterfield

(Dream Journal 3:30 a.m.)

I had a dream in which everything knew
who they were
and I was a painter, the pen reminded
me of what I didn't say in a
dream I couldn't remember. Walls still
too thick to hear through and I am the only
one in the class that knew that logic didn't
make sense. Who am I?

Blackness knew
who I was and our methylated genes from Agent Orange.
Maybe there were elephants in the jungle and I
hadn't spent my allowance yet. That is how
dreams appear when you are everything you already are.

War Supporters
Jim Marney-Petix

"Greetings. Your friends and neighbors have chosen you…" It's possibly the most unpopular opening line in the history of America. I really hated my "friends and neighbors." Not only because they were ultimately the reason I was in Vietnam but because they wouldn't talk to me when I got back. All too often, I'd get five minutes of small talk from the people who supported the war, then off to important business on the other side of the room. Based on their behavior, I got the impression that they were embarrassed. They reminded me of fair-weather football fans who can't say enough good things about a team that's winning but don't want to talk about a team that's not. I felt judged. Something along the lines of, "If you couldn't win the war, then you can't be much of a man." Or perhaps, "Please don't go crazy and shoot up the party until after I've left." Absolutely no indication of willingness to talk about my military experience or its effect on me.

In fairness, I wasn't too eager to open up to them either. Part of it was male mystique; a real man just didn't ask for help. Part of it was the feeling that we were trying to communicate from different universes. They kept talking about me being in fear for my life. That was why I was having a bad reaction to my wartime experiences. That was why I was depressed, and couldn't concentrate, and had bad dreams. It neatly explained all the bad things that were happening to me. The problem was that it just wasn't true. Of course, I was in fear for my life early on, but I got used to it. It was like driving on the freeway, intrinsically dangerous, but after a while, I just didn't think about it.

The real reason I was having a bad reaction to my wartime experience was that I was afraid I was a monster, and the last thing I needed was to talk about it and have them confirm my fears by running screaming into the night. Also, I was feeling guilty because, although I was scared, I was home; and there were better soldiers, better human beings behind me that would never come home. I did not deserve to be here; they did not deserve being there.

The stuff I really needed to talk about was dark and depressing, and nobody wanted to go there. So, it was all platitudes and safe subjects. Hell, I could understand that; I wasn't going to press it. But it was more than that. It felt like I was no longer part of their world. Like I was a broken "other." As a war hero, I was someone they knew they should respect and honor, but they wanted to do it from a safe distance.

I went to war so others wouldn't have to. That's the way it works. Unless the war is so total that enemy soldiers are invading your hometown, some are chosen to go and bear the cost of the fighting so that the rest can be insulated from the brutal reality and carry on with their lives. If it's for the people I love, that's exactly the way I want it to work. And if the rest of the country got a free ride at my expense, I didn't mind.

But when I came home, there was a wall between us. There was just so much that could not be shared that I had no community to go home to. I felt like Frodo Baggins at the end of the movie version of The Lord Of The Rings. After a year of hardship and blood, pain and gore, loss and guilt, I'd returned to the Green Dragon, where the talk was about prize pumpkins, this year's harvest, and a cow that's wandered into a neighbor's garden. Where do I go from here?

War Protesters
Jim Marney-Petix

I could have done without the name-calling and hostility. On the other hand, they were willing to talk about the war when most of the rest of the population just wouldn't. Of course, some of these "talks" were actually shouting matches, but an argument can also be a conversation. At the time, I didn't agree with most of what they said, but I came to see them as an honorable enemy. They were out on the streets protesting a war they thought completely wrongheaded and facing massive retaliation for it, up to and including live fire. They were beaten, arrested, lost their citizenship, and were occasionally killed. I could respect that. In fact, I admired them so much that I married one.

She supported me for two years while I finished my B.S. in Entomology. She nursed me through my deepest periods of depression. She shepherded me through a period when I was seriously suicidal. And she talked me down from an episode that would have had me in jail for the rest of my life if it had taken its natural course.

In my mid to late thirties, I learned that my work-obsessed, autocratic father had had a secret life as a child molester, and apparently, my sisters were some of his victims. Fortunately, I had no idea where to find him because, for about three days, I had to actively talk myself out of trying to kill him. My wife talked me down by pointing out that nothing I did to him would benefit my sisters; their damage was already done, and I would definitely destroy the rest of my life in the process.

The other thing that forced me to keep a lid on it and get my emotions back under control was my conviction that if I tried to kill him, I would surely succeed. This was Arizona; guns were everywhere. I grew up with them and knew them inside and out. More importantly, I was a combat veteran; I knew exactly how to do it. Not just the technical knowledge of calibers, high-value targets, setting up the ambush, minimizing collateral damage, and so on, but most importantly, I knew how to take on the mindset. How do I take a man I used to love and respect and turn him into a dangerous object?

The trouble with knowing something is that there is no way to unknow it. The scars on my mind are just as permanent as the scars on my body. I keep the monster within me locked in a steel vault, but I have to live with the fact that it will always be there.

This marriage lasted fifteen years. It fell apart because I was trying to cheat on her. I don't know why. I didn't even know what I wanted or what I was trying to accomplish. I broke up a good marriage to a splendid woman for no reason I understand.

pOETRY

Drown out the truth of the past
(what you say is nothing).
Only the shoulder blades that
carried water can tell me
what to remember; what was
too heavy to carry.

Men and women cry when the
soldier in them returns
forgetting what to say, what to
remember, the womb-men carry.

You did what you could, but there
is no poetry in politics.
Then how can you take credit when the earth
and grass try to cover up a Sandberg,
and my tissue paper is a book marker
for the sorrow of war is what I carry.

Sacrifice

Jim Marney-Petix

We do it so the people we love don't have to.

We place ourselves in harm's way.

We decorate our bodies with scars.

We live through the pain.

All this we do willingly.

Hoping we are the only ones.

Quiet Patriotism
G. Craige Edgerton

An unseen storm hides in the canyons and chasms
Of a mind in denial. Not a storm
Of flashes and roars, but one hidden
Subtle and obscure, waiting to pounce
Out of a calm, serene, inspirational moment.
Memorial Day, 2022.

Songs, banners, and hoopla all around.
The boob tube explodes with sugary patriotism.
Tears and cheers coax me to trust, draw me in
And I almost believe it.

My unseen storm of avoidance, anger, resentment
Swirls, tornado-like, out into the open, battling with
Waving flags, bejeweled generals,
Red, White, and Blue dripping from every pore.

I want to be patriotic, wave the flag
Wear my outfit's hat, have God Bless America,
Pledge my allegiance and actually mean it.

But I can't. Not that kind of patriotism
That is borne of righteousness: me better than them,
Superior because of being born in the right place.

My patriotism is quiet.
No flags, no medals, no cheers at artificial parades.
No banners, no singing, no saluting.
And damn sure, no guns or rocket's red glare.

The backbone of true patriotism
Is the genuine greeting, the sincere compliment,
The helping hand, the encouraging word
That lifts both.

I cannot accept the syrupy driveling of jingoistic nationalism.
I can accept quietly, without fanfare, with no parade or pomp,
In any circumstance, try to make the world just a little better
Every day.

The Plan
Jim Marney-Petix

I was working in Redwood City on Seaport Blvd. and living in north Fremont near Mission and Niles Canyon Rd. My second wife and I were still together. So, it must have been early to mid-90s, and I was suicidal. There was no other way to put it. I was in so much pain that I would have done anything to stop it. And I was convinced that it would be like this forever. I had a plan worked out in considerable detail.

Method: Single car accident, late at night, on the way home from work. I had a favorite sushi house in Redwood City where I intended to take a late supper and drink far too much sake before driving home.

Location: Between Seaport Blvd and Marsh Rd in Redwood City is a freeway frontage road called East Bayshore Rd that runs straight for about 1/2 to 1 mile before it abruptly turns north to become Haven Ave before joining Hwy 84 and eventually crossing the Dumbarton Bridge. South of East Bayshore Rd is Hwy 101's sound wall just a few feet away. Where East Bayshore Rd abruptly turns north, the freeway sound wall also abruptly turns north for about 20-30 feet before turning east again. So anyone driving east on East Bayshore Rd would find the sound wall directly in front at a sharp left turn. The sound wall had no guard rail in front of it, just an ordinary curb.

Time: Monday night was an 'all you can eat' sushi bar. I figured I'd get there about 8:00 and leave about 9:00 or 10:00. At that time of night East Bayshore Rd has essentially no traffic. The road in front of the wall was straight and long enough for me to get my car going as fast as it could go. I didn't intend to have my seatbelt fastened.

PTSD
Bill Noyes

Memorial Day brings vibrant blooms,
Again, I see with a vacant stare.
Where colors cloak the fields of graves
I see, again, the ground unturned.

If he, not me. I know he knows the
Answer to my question: why?
A billowing bloom as life must leave,
To let another's future bloom.

As I go right he left this world.
His quickened step went down a path toward doom.
No surprise, no thrill in war achieved!
Just death revealed in a thousand scenes.

Helping A Brother Out
Jaime Lee Johnson

While having lunch with a friend, he asked me if I had been going to the VA for services or help. I told him I tried years ago, but nothing came of it. It didn't help that the psychiatrist had no concept or understanding of the differences between the National Guard and Reserves.

After a bit of back and forth, he gave me the name of someone at a place called the Vet Center. I called them a few days later. Other than having enlisted into the US Army infantry, it was the best decision I have ever made. It probably saved my life.

The Little Box
G. Craige Edgerton

They're kept in a box in a drawer,
Behind the socks, under key and locks.
Never to see bright truth and light
Or the dazzling moon at midnight.

A secret so dark and deep
It cannot creep or seep into
The conscious stream of thought
No matter how sincerely sought.

Inscribed on the little box,
In fine script, lettered in gold,
The words that have haunted
His soul's threshold:

"MORAL INJURY"

Hidden for 50 years behind
Streams of tears and rivers of fears
And too many beers
To drown the unheard cheers
Or the screaming, virulent, nasty jeers.

They say his service was grand,
That he stood up; he made a stand.
He was a man!
But the talk was bland,
And grinded like sand
On the palm of his hand.

For this, he had not planned.

It's safe in the box,
Like the cliffs holding rocks.
Never to open or share.
For this he would not dare.

A peek into the hidden container
Was encouraged by his mindful trainer.
What's to lose if he were to open
A concealed little box for just a moment.

He dreamed and schemed that night,
Of the fearsome fright
Of the might of that hidden little box.
So long forgotten, so long out of sight.

I can; I will; I can't; I won't
Back and forth; fear and hope
Pulling and tugging and twisting and turning
And spinning his churning doubtful mind.

The tiny voice of knowing,
Battling the screaming voice of fear.
David vs Goliath penetrates
His mind, so unclear, so austere.

To open or not to open
That is the fear.
To be free from doubt
To open the box and let the secret out?

Holding the box with trepidation
Hands sweating, fearing damnation,

But steadfast in determination,
The lid slowly lifts and reveals…salvation!

The shame, the guilt, the anger and embarrassment
Fly forth from the hidden little box.
To dissipate into air
Like steam out of volcanic rocks

The box IS the block.
But only in the mind of fear and doubt
And avoidance and the unknown.
All in that little box in the drawer behind the socks.

The box is the block,
And too, the box is the opening.
Box-block; box-open
Box-open; box block.

A long, strange trip with that little box.
Avoidance, anger, resentment, regret, moral injury.
All wrapped up, neat and tidy,
And tucked away in such a tiny little box.

The voice of truth and courage finally prevails.
The box of avoidance is opened to reveal,
An uplifting tale of duty, honor, service, and pride
That now rests in the box, lid open wide.

The dreams and themes and schemes and screams
We all make and break and forsake and take as truth,
Are only the stories we make up,
And put away in a hidden little box.

What's in your little box?

Homeless Bum
Sunny "Dos" Dosanjh

I sat on the concrete next to a homeless bum
in front of a liquor store
I didn't realize the homeless bum was me.

We both laughed out loud as the sun hit us
squarely across our weather-beaten faces
Time stood still and everything was ok

Another homeless bum appeared out of the light
He was smiling with the few teeth he had left

What a motley crew we turned out to be
No direction, No place, No particular hurry

The sun had moved on a bit
So it was my turn to give up my persona

I got up…smiled and took my leave
I don't think I'll ever see them again

But nonetheless, the homeless bum
that was seated is now standing

It's a start that I do not look forward to
Society is lost in the paper chase

It's easier and friendlier
When I'm a homeless bum

At least I know what is True.

Chapter III
Mending Fences

"The true soldier fights not because he hates what is in front of him but because he loves what is behind him."
—G.K. Chesterton

A father and son work to repair the back fence after a storm. They sit and talk after a job well done. In an unexplained moment, healing occurs.

This is a true event shared by one of the veteran writers. It was a perfect example of recovery, redemption, and forgiveness. Sometimes, healing can be a long, arduous process. Other times, it can happen unexpectedly, in a moment.

Two main themes run through Mending Fences: Tapestry and Kintsugi. Although not explicitly referred to in each writing, readers can better understand this chapter by considering these two themes as they read.

Tapestry is the weaving of materials together with fine thread. In this case, the materials are experiences of the veteran's life. Each Tapestry becomes a unique work of art for that writer. Those Tapestries are combined to create this book, which becomes a Tapestry of Tapestries.

One of the writers discovered that if he were to reduce all of his writings to one word, it would be Kintsugi, the Japanese art of mending broken pottery with a lacquer mixture of gold, silver, or platinum. Mended pottery is an apt metaphor for these mended veterans.

This chapter deals with how these veterans have sought healing or at least attempted to deal with their PTSD or trauma. The process doesn't have an ending, but progress can be made with proper guidance.

Hopefully, these writings open possibilities for the reader or their loved one and give them <u>Permission to Walk in Peace.</u>

Mending Fences
Sunny "Dos" Dosanjh

The atmospheric river rainfall had done a number on our backyard fence. Pieces of wood lay scattered and the fence looked battered. Dad, who is approaching 80 years, surveyed the damage and brought out his toolbox. His tools were a hodgepodge of items that he'd collected over the years.

And so, it began.

He gathered a few odd bits and pieces of wood, sawed a few into shape and began the repairs. I had been making a plain omelet, thrown onto a couple of pieces of bread, and asked Dad if he wanted a sandwich.

He said "yes" and also asked for a glass of water.

I put the food outside and he first asked me to help with the repairs.

"No problem," I said and got busy.

There we were, father and son, mending fences.

The fence still looked battered but now it was held together with a few odd-shaped pieces of wood. It did the job.

We both sat down next to the fence and ate our omelet sandwiches. He kept the bread crusts for an old crow that visited us each day. We talked slowly about the simple things in life, like bread and water. We sat quietly for a while until he raised a memory about his Grandfather and Grandmother. They were from the late 1800's and he described how they lived off the land and were grateful for whatever the good lord provided.

As he spoke, he looked at me.

Here I was, a broken spirit and had lost everything, essentially a disappointment in his eyes.

He had high hopes for me. Instead, against his wishes, I joined the Military, but I came back from service as a shell of my former self. There were a few moments of joy, but overall, I was living a life of failure, after failure, after failure.

I eventually hit rock bottom, then the bottom gave out.

To catch me as I fell, was my Dad.

He looked at me and said, "Good job on the fence."

It was in that moment that a spark was lit and I could "see" my Dad.

He was a simple man, from humble beginnings and did the best he could. Now here we sat, looking at the broken and fragmented pieces of my life, and his light was shining on me. I saw the broken man that I had become, yet I knew I was not alone.

A doorway was shown to me telling me to start picking up the tattered pieces of my life and start fixing them. I don't know from where or why the storm had decided to batter our fence. But it provided us an opportunity to see "eye-to-eye" and start a dialogue to understand each other.

The old crow had finished munching on the bread crusts and flew away. What he left behind were two men, starting to mend a relationship while mending fences.

Tapestry
G. Craige Edgerton

I weave a newfound tapestry
As I return to Vietnam.
Two score and fifteen years
I've waited for…what?

A tapestry of hope
A new fabric in my mind
The old tapestry worn and frayed.
Slowly disposed of and retired.

Tangled strings and mesh
Thoughts and feelings spinning
In the loom of my mind
Begins to build a new tapestry.

A thread of emotion—red
A strand like fear—black
Anticipation and angst—yellow
Hope and redemption—green

A new tapestry emerges
Born in forgiveness
By Vietnamese brothers.
Can I now forgive myself?
My new tapestry holds the key.

I've always thought about what it might be like to return to Vietnam after I served there in the Marine Corps in 1969. The opportunity arose in 2024 through Veterans For Peace # 160, an organization that takes veterans back to Vietnam for various personal reasons and provides charitable support for multiple non-profits doing good for the citizens of Vietnam negatively impacted by the war. Over the 55 years since I left, I have woven a tapestry of my experiences in my memory that has become my reality. I am searching for a new story about my time there by weaving a new tapestry. This is the story of that journey and how it impacted me.

When I chose to return to Vietnam after 55 years, I did so with no expectations. Or so I thought. The truth is that I did have some deeply held expectations. I hoped to find closure for my guilt about the damage I caused while there in the Marine Corps in 1969. I have been in counseling for almost 8 years, and although I have made significant progress, I have not come to complete peace with it. I have described the healing process to my counselor as peeling back layers of an onion, trying to get to its core. I was looking for that core in my return to Vietnam.

I've always thought about what it might be like to return to Vietnam after I served there in the Marine Corps in 1969. The opportunity arose in 2024 through Veterans For Peace # 160, an organization that takes veterans back to Vietnam for various personal reasons and provides charitable support for multiple non-profits doing good for the citizens of Vietnam negatively impacted by the war. Over the 55 years since I left, I have woven a tapestry of my experiences in my memory that has become my reality. I am searching for a new story about my time there by weaving a new tapestry. This is the story of that journey and how it impacted me. When I chose to return to Vietnam after 55 years, I did so with no expectations. Or so I thought.

The truth is that I did have some deeply held expectations. I hoped to find closure for my guilt about the damage I caused while there in the Marine Corps in 1969. I have been in counseling for almost 8 years, and although I have made significant progress, I have not come to complete peace with it. I have described the healing process to my counselor as peeling back layers of an onion, trying to get to its core. I was looking for that core in my return to Vietnam.

I had no idea what that core looked or smelled like. I wasn't sure the core was even there or that it existed. But I was willing to be open to the possibility that the location of the core of the guilt might be the place where it began. Thus, my return.

One of my first impressions was from a barista in a local coffee house in Ha Noi. After ordering the strong Vietnamese coffee, he overheard our group talking and recognized the American English. After a polite introduction, he said, "I want you to remember Vietnam is a country; Vietnam is not a war." That statement contained so much more than just the words, and it became a theme throughout our trip.

The Children Broke the Ice

The first 3 days were spent in Ha Noi, the capital city of the old North Vietnam and also the capital of the newly reunified Vietnam. For most of the time since Vietnam had been in my consciousness, Ha Noi was a profanity not to be spoken in polite society. It conjured up visions of the home of a violent, repressive communist dictatorship, a puppet of the Chinese who were bent on taking over the world with their repressive form of government, and the lair of the notorious Ho Chi Minh, Uncle Ho, as he was known. It was also the home of those trying to kill me. Just saying the name Ha Noi sent chills up my back.

The first night in Ha Noi I was anxious to get out and see Vietnam for the first time since I left exactly 55 years ago, in October 1969. A few of us strolled a short distance to Hoan Kiem Lake, the sacred center of Ha Noi, and all of Vietnam. It just so happened to be the 70th anniversary of the defeat of the French at Dien Bien Phu, and the lake was alive with music, celebrations, women in their Ao Dais taking photos, and generally, all having a good time. It was mostly family-oriented with no rowdiness.

As we sauntered around, I was surprised to hear a very friendly Vietnamese woman in her mid-twenties call to me. "Mr., Mr.! Mr. American. Can you help me?" With two kids in tow, a girl and a boy, both about 8 or 9 years old, and all 3 well dressed, she asked, "Sir, can you help the children with English speaking?" Huh? I was caught off guard and suspected it was some kind of hook that would lead to requests for money.

But my skepticism soon turned to absolute joy. Each child had a list of questions, pre-printed on what looked like a school homework lesson, that they asked in English and wanted a response in English. I was beside myself, as I was more excited than the kids. I learned later that all kids are required to learn English in school, and talking to Americans is a standard practice.

It was noisy with the celebration, and they had very soft voices. With my poor hearing, I had to stoop over to try to hear and understand their broken English. Where are you from? What is your favorite color? Do you have children? It continued until all 10 questions and answers were completed—in English!

But we all managed, and they filled out their homework sheet, and I filled my heart. It was my first night back in Vietnam, and the children broke the ice. The hope in their faces created a gold thread that was the beginning of my new tapestry!

We Don't Forget

For the next few days, I found myself walking the streets of a peaceful, albeit busy and noisy city, not unlike most large cities of the world. People were going about their lives, working, playing, and raising their families, much like in America. I, as an oversized human compared to the diminutive Vietnamese, was pretty much ignored, just another tourist. There was no animosity, no sideways glances, no sneering. Nothing. What? Where's the anger? Where's the grief? Where's the hatred? What the hell is going on here?

As I strolled, I couldn't help but remember the few times I

interacted with the local Vietnamese while here for the first time. My experience then was of people going about their lives as best they could, many not understanding why the Americans were here in the first place. I was fully aware that some of them were Viet Cong, but I also understood that many were not. The similarity between then and now was striking. It took a few days of interacting with the people of Ha Noi to realize that the war was over for them. Done with. Finished. They got over it and are moving forward. They forgive us. Believe them...they really do FORGIVE US. It was me that couldn't get over it.

"We forgive, but we don't forget," she whispered, her stern look drilling into my soul through her eyes. "Remember that!", she said as she slipped away. We had just finished hearing a speech by Dr. Phan Anh Son of the Vietnam Union of Friendship Organizations touting the success of the communist revolution and its glorious future. I posed the following question to the government bureaucrat: "Do you think that, in the long run, a communist government can coexist with a free market capitalist economy?" His answer was rather obtuse but sincere in his belief that they could indeed coexist. He was adamant in adding that they could not only coexist but it was the perfect model for the future success of Vietnam.

But my question was not one that any Vietnamese could ask without some possible repercussions. I sensed that it created some discomfort, and the woman who had approached me wanted to inform me in her very determined manner that this form of government was working just fine and better than what the Americans tried to force on them some 50 or so years ago. I think she was insulted that I would even consider the possibility of failure of the current Vietnamese system and even rude to bring it up. At least that's how I interpreted it.

Later on, I asked Chuck, the President of VFP #160, who had lived in Vietnam since 1992, if my assessment was true and if my question would be, at a minimum, frowned upon by the government. He said it was partially true. There is a line the citizens understand cannot be crossed. It is not clearly defined but understood by almost all. I asked him if the newspapers could criticize the government, and he said they could, to a certain point, as long as they didn't step over that same undefined line. The woman was giving me a not-so-subtle warning that my question was inappropriate. I had stepped over that unclear line. A dark strand of yarn was added to my tapestry.

Lost Brothers

A new green thread (for their uniform color) was added to my tapestry when I had some interactions with Vietnamese soldiers. As we stepped off the bus to visit the Ho Chi Minh Museum in Ha Noi, we were greeted by a handful of older Vietnamese soldiers who were veterans of the American War. They were in full uniform and exceedingly proud. I was surprised by the vigorous handshaking and patting us on the back. It was as though we were long-lost brothers, and in a way, we were.

We couldn't communicate with them through language, but we made a genuine connection through our eyes and smiles. The interaction lasted just a few minutes, but a real camaraderie existed. I wish I could sit down with them and get more details about where they served, their jobs, and how they felt about American veterans returning 55 years later. I will cherish that first interaction with Vietnamese soldiers as another strand in my tapestry.

Captain to Captain

Later that day, we visited the Vietnam Friendship Village Project USA, founded in 1998 by returning American war veterans. Today, it serves up to 120 disabled children who live at the Project with educational and vocational training. In addition, it provides respite for Vietnamese war veterans from the American war. As we completed the tour of the children's area, our guide, Gioi, excitedly let us know that he had a surprise for us.

A contingent of Vietnamese war veterans, mostly women, served together in the same unit fighting against the Americans. They had kept in contact, and this was a reunion. There were about a dozen of them, and they were just as surprised to see us as we were to see them. Neither was expecting the other. We all gathered in a room, sitting in a circle.

Our interpreter, Hung, explained to both groups why we were all here, both American veterans and Vietnamese veterans. Through Hung we began to ask questions of one another. I could see the suspicion on their faces and their reluctance to communicate with us at first. But eventually, they relaxed as they understood more about us.

One gentleman seemed to be the spokesman for the Vietnamese group, and after a few questions and answers, we discovered he was their unit's captain. It dawned on me that I was also a captain and the only officer in the group from the U.S. After a few hesitant moments, I asked Hung to explain that I, too, was a captain and asked if I could shake his hand. The Vietnamese captain was reluctant at first as he didn't understand the request. But Hung persisted, and he eventually understood.

I stood and approached the area between the two groups. The Vietnamese captain did the same, and we shook hands. Even though he still seemed suspicious, he accepted my handshake, and we smiled together in a reconciliation moment. This was a continuation of my desire to connect with Vietnamese soldiers on a one-to-one basis, even if we couldn't communicate directly. This was another moment in my reconciliation of my time in Vietnam so many years ago.

The Salute

On the fourth day, we departed for Da Nang and Hoi An, about 180 km south of the Demilitarized Zone (DMZ), in Quang Tri Province, the most northerly province in the old South Vietnam and my home for seven months in 1969. Dong Ha was the village where the Marine Corps' most northerly combat base was. One of my jobs was to be in charge of a 4.2-inch mortar battery to protect the perimeter of that base. It was my home for a few of those 7 months, and I wanted to see how much it had changed.

As I returned to Quang Tri Province, I was filled with questions. How different will it be? Will I recognize anything? What memories will come rushing back? Is it anxiety I feel or excitement? Will I get triggered by bad memories? Will I embrace an area where I caused so much destruction? Can I find forgiveness for myself and the Vietnamese people? And on and on...

On the bus ride north from Hue, I could feel the energy building in me. Was it real, or was I creating something that was not there? I came to Vietnam because I initially saw on the itinerary that one stop was Dong Ha and Leatherneck Square. That's where I served in 1969. I wanted to go back and see what awaited me, if anything.

Quang Tri City today is not what I left in 1969. It was almost leveled in the Tet Offensive in 1968 and completely destroyed in another battle in 1972. It has been totally rebuilt in the past 55 years with mostly all-new infrastructure and more updated homes. On the surface, there appears to be no remembrance of the American war. But on deeper inspection, remnants remain.

But even more importantly, I wanted to see if I could tap into any energy from so long ago. I don't know exactly what I was looking for, but I felt something was waiting for me. I was not disappointed.

In Quang Tri, we met with a local politician who was a long-time friend of Chuck Searcy and the co-founder of Project RENEW, Chuck's signature charitable program in Vietnam. After a lengthy conversation between Chuck and the Vietnamese officials, in which praise was showered on one another, as was Vietnamese custom, the floor was opened for questions.

By this time, I was fully engaged in the friendship and camaraderie shown to us. I wanted to interact directly with a Vietnamese soldier or veteran. I asked if any veterans of the American war were present as I'd like to shake their hand. None were, but one of the officials sitting next to the main politician started to answer in Vietnamese. The interpreter informed me that he was a veteran but not of the American war. Eventually, I learned he was a retired 2 star general and president of the Vietnamese Veterans Association. This was the type of soldier I wanted to meet.

Because I had asked the question, he welcomed me personally after finishing his rather lengthy answer and then sat down. I was across the large table, stood up, and asked if he would stand again. As he stood, I saluted him, and he saluted me back. Brother to brother. I held it together, but just barely. This was another giant step toward redemption and a beautiful green thread to add to my new **tapestry**.

Later that day, we traveled to the Troung Son National Military Cemetery (equivalent to Arlington National Cemetery in the U.S.) to assist the Vietnamese Veterans Association in laying a wreath and placing incense in the main Pagoda. It was a solemn ceremony with the Vietnamese National Anthem, speeches, and music. We were invited to participate and walked side-by-side with the Vietnamese soldiers in full military regalia with medals and all. The same general that I saluted earlier in the day was there and the highest ranking member.

I shook his hand and connected with him more intimately than over the giant table previously. Although he was too young to have served in the American War, he was deployed against Pol Pot in 1979, then sent to the China border to fight China's nasty incursion meant to punish the Vietnamese for attacking their Cambodian ally and to draw off two divisions from Cambodia.

He was exceedingly proud of his service and the high rank he had achieved. It was another moment of realization of the insanity of war. I was shaking the hand of my dreaded enemy, and neither of us held enmity toward one another. My tapestry was growing in complexity.

Rin

The centerpiece of the **tapestry** was about to be woven in, and I was unprepared for it. In Quang Tri, we visited the home of a Vietnamese family in Gio Linh Township with a child born with severe disabilities, the result of exposure to Agent Orange. He was 29 years old, had never had mobility nor control of his body, was unable to speak, and required full-time care. His parents were very poor, and the mother could not work as she was his full-time caretaker.

The home was barely livable by American standards and modest even by rural Vietnamese standards. But it was clean, orderly, and functional for this very poor family. We were given a summary of this family's situation before arriving, but no level of preparation was adequate for what we found.

The young man, Nguyen Duc Rin, was on a concrete platform with a small pad and blanket beneath him. I guessed it was for sanitary purposes as he had no control of bodily functions. He could roll his head with only minimal control, and although he tried to focus his eyes, it was almost impossible. After a short introduction from the mother, she invited us to visit her son.

One person in our group, Tony, was a long-term nurse and immediately stepped forward to interact with Rin. The rest of us held back, not sure what to do. I found it hard to see this person as someone I could communicate with. I had only one other close encounter with a young girl in California in a similar situation, and although severe, she was more functional than Rin.

A couple of others took turns, one at a time, approaching him, holding his hand, saying a few comforting words (which he couldn't understand because of his disabilities, and we spoke English), and trying to make any possible connection. As he rolled his eyes and head, he appeared pleased with our visit. His mother had given us clues about his reactions and said that she could communicate with him only through his eyes.

I was reluctant at first to approach him. But a little voice inside my head asked: "Isn't this why you came to Vietnam? What are you afraid of? Get over there and connect with that young man. There is a gift for you in doing so." I recognized the voice and trusted it. I approached him with almost reverence, not understanding why. After all, it was just one human connecting with another one. But it turned out to be much more than that.

His hand waved back and forth with no control. I took it and held it for a few seconds. It was very soft as he had never been able to use it. He rolled his eyes, trying to find me and focus. Eventually, he was able to stabilize them, and we connected. The deformities seemed to disappear as I looked deeply into his eyes. There was a moment when we seemed to know each other, or at least I could see him as a person, not his deformities. I'll never know what he was thinking or if he could even have thoughts. All I can hope for is that he experienced some connection with me, too.

I whispered a few words and thanked him for the deep connection that I experienced. With that, his eyes rolled back, and we lost the eye-to-eye connection. I gently squeezed his hand once more and left the room. As I slowly returned to the group in the other room, I was overcome with emotion. I was not crying but basking in a deep personal connection that I have rarely experienced. Something had happened to me, and I didn't understand it. I looked for a place to sit down and found a small cinder block wall.

I sat down as my knees were about to abandon me. Jan could see the stress on my face and came to sit next to me. That's when it hit. I placed my face in the palms of my hands, eyes closed, to try and steady myself. A scene suddenly appeared in my mind that I was not prepared for.

I was on a firebase like the ones I was on my first time in Vietnam. It was a bare hilltop with 105 MM howitzers lined up in formation. It was hot and dusty, and sand-bagged bunkers were spread throughout. Large, bright white flashes, like flashbulbs in old cameras, were going off all around, and for just a moment, I was back in 1969. There was no sound, and no other Marines were seen. It was just me standing alone, observing the flashing lights on that firebase. The scene was vivid, and I felt like I was there, not as an observer, but as a participant. It only lasted a second or two but the intensity of it was stamped into my mind's eye. I don't think I can ever forget those few moments.

As the scene disappeared, I had to pause momentarily and try to understand what had just happened. I had no clue. It was completely unexpected and unplanned. That is when I started to weep silently at first and then more intensely. What did it mean? Where did it come from? Why did it so impact me? I know it is important but what do I do with it? The emotions rolled over and through me, and I let it be whatever it was. I didn't try to stop it, control it, or figure out what it was. For the time being, I let it be. I'd figure out the meaning in due time.

Jan placed her hand on my leg to let me know she was there, and I started to regain my sense of place. For that short moment, I had traveled to another time, another place. The message was received but yet to be interpreted. I knew that if I let it be, the meaning would reveal itself in time.

Mickey sat down on the other side of me from Jan and placed his hand on my shoulder. He had served in the same area at about the same time as me, and even though he didn't understand exactly what had happened in my mind, he understood the impact on me. There is a bond with comrades in arms that is hard to explain but is real. He was feeling the emotion with me. We met each other's eyes, and nothing more needed to be said. We both understood.

Lou, another veteran who was not in combat, also came over and touched my shoulder. I gladly accepted his offer of support as I looked up at him. His innate compassion touched me and helped me get grounded. I tried to get up and join the rest of the group but wasn't quite ready. I remained sitting on the short wall, trying to find meaning in the intense experience I had just had.

What was that all about? The location and time were obvious, but why did it come right after meeting with the Agent Orange victim, Rin? What was the connection, if any? I trusted that little knowing voice inside me would eventually help me understand. As I sat there asking the questions, I began to get the answer. The young man represented all my guilt, anger, remorse, embarrassment, shame, and any other negative feelings I had about my time and place in the war. He held all that for me, and by connecting through our eyes, he forgave me, which allowed me to release all those old feelings. I heard: "It's okay. We all forgive you." And for the first time in over 55 years, I understood. If he could forgive me after what we had done to him, it was time for me to forgive myself.

When I realized the importance of what had happened, I could feel the release in my body. It felt like a long overdue shower washing away all the baggage I had been carrying for so long. And that is when the tears really started to flow. The tears became a shower, washing away the hurt I had hauled around all these years. That hurt had become a part of me. Fifty-five years washed away in less than a few minutes. I was weaving a new **tapestry** with fresh yellow yarn and a different picture of forgiveness and redemption. And this young, disfigured man was at the center of that new **tapestry**.

Trying to explain this profound experience rationally is beyond me. I am not a psychologist and do not understand how the mind works in situations like this. However, I have life experience and know that seemingly unrelated events can catalyze change. I had made up a story, true or not, about my time in Vietnam, and it took connecting with this young man to allow me to make up a different story. I recognized that I was seeking a new story. I was ready for any possibility. Without that intention on my part, I doubt I would have been able to recognize the new story being presented to me.

Initially, I said I had no expectations for this trip, but I soon realized I did. This event was the central expectation I had. I wanted to find closure to all my hurt and pain for so many years and I found it in a severely impacted victim of Agent Orange. That is not how I expected it to unfold, but I was ready because I focused my intention. And I'm so glad I was!

I'm sure I will never see Rin again, but he is forever in my heart. I wish I could share my experience with him and tell him how much he meant to me. I plan to reconnect with him by providing help for his family through VFP #160. Thank you, Rin!

Firebase Fuller

Meeting this young man was not the last of my more profound experiences. I had multiple insights throughout the trip that all seemed to roll into one large impression of the Vietnamese people today. The courtesy required to maneuver all those motorbikes through crowded streets without crashing into one another said a lot about the Vietnamese culture of politeness. The ease with which Vietnamese teenagers would look at us as tourists, smile and say "hello". That is not common in the U.S. It is expected that those in the service industry would be polite and accommodating. Still, I experienced that same friendliness in areas unrelated to the tourist trade, which showed their true nature. The Vietnamese people truly are generous, polite, friendly, and gracious. Their overall gentle nature provided a stunning backdrop for my new **tapestry**.

One last experience provided the final reconciliation and did not directly involve the Vietnamese people. I had hoped, from the beginning, to visit one of the actual sites where I had been deployed. I knew it was a long shot, but I still wanted to go. I mentioned this to some of the other veterans in my group back in San Jose, and they thought I was crazy. They said they never wanted to see or come near any location they had previously been to. However, I felt a strong pull to see, or at least get near, one of my firebases.

On the last day in Quang Tri province, we followed Hwy 9 west out of Dong Ha to the famous battlefield of Khe Sanh. That ferocious battle lasted 77 days, starting in January 1968. There were many casualties on both sides, and it was a key moment that changed the attitude about the U.S. presence in Vietnam. Today, it is a historical site with a museum, a field of airplanes, helicopters, tanks, and remnants of the American base that was eventually abandoned.

Our guide, Hien, grew up in this remote northwest corner of Vietnam. As I talked to him, he mentioned that he and his friends collected scrap metal from some of the firebases near his home. Knowing we were near some of my firebases, I asked if he knew any by name.

"Sure", he said. "We used to go to Fuller quite a lot".

"Fuller?" I exclaimed. "That was one of my firebases! Can you point it out?"

"Yes, we passed it on the way here. On the way back, I'll show it to you."

I couldn't believe it. I had found one of my firebases. To say I was excited would be a gross understatement. Highway 9, the road we took to Khe Sanh, is a modern paved road today. But in 1969, it was a dirt road used by the U.S. military and South Vietnamese forces to access the Ho Chi Minh Trail in Laos.

As the trees along the road parted, he had the bus driver pull over.

"Look up there," Hien said, pointing to a distant hilltop. "That is Fuller."

He was pointing to a distant hill, about ½ mile away and about 1,000 feet in elevation. It was different from the surrounding hilltops because it was flat on top. To create a firebase, engineers would come into a hilltop after the Marines had secured it, flattening it with heavy equipment, which allowed a 105 MM howitzer battery to be installed.

I just stared at it, not knowing what to say. *Firebase Fuller!* I couldn't take my eyes off of it. Here I was 55 years later, looking at one of my firebases. I never would have recognized it because I looked up, not down like in 1969. I didn't feel anger, sadness, remorse, or any other negative feelings. It was like returning to the town you grew up in and haven't seen in over 50 years. It is the same town, but it looks and feels completely different. *Firebase Fuller!* I was absolutely amazed!

As I continued staring at it, I told the others it was one of the places I served when I was there. I think I said it a few times while trying to convince myself that it was real. The impact of seeing it and being so near was another healing moment. Seeing it peaceful and quiet released much of my negative feelings about my time here. My memories of Fuller were of a desolate place full of constant activity and threats from the enemy. Now, I could replace that image of a peaceful remote hilltop returning to its proper place in the jungle. A beautiful green strand of yarn was added to my new **tapestry**.

My New Tapestry

The opening words of this piece were, "I've always wondered what it might be like to return to Vietnam after I served there in the Marine Corps in 1969." Now I know. After just over 2 weeks in Vietnam, I was exposed to all I had hoped for and much more. I left Vietnam in October 1969 and was deployed to Okinawa. In November, I was sent home for my mom's funeral. From that time forward, I carried an invisible flak jacket of negative feelings, trying my best never to let anyone know I had served in Vietnam, much less in the Marine Corps.

Although I have a productive and peaceful life, the weight of that flak jacket was a lifelong burden. I was not aware of it most of the time but the discomfort of it occasionally seeped into my awareness.

In Vietnam last month, I removed and retired the flak jacket. I loosened it as I met the Vietnamese people, especially the soldiers. Each time I was able to shake hands with one of them, the flak jacket became a little lighter. Meeting Rin, the Agent Orange victim, allowed me to slip one arm out. The final removal came when I saw Firebase Fuller. As I stared at it, I had a physical sensation of release, of the flak jacket slipping off my shoulders and falling to the floor. **Vietnam of 1969 no longer had a grip on me.**

Today, I still haven't chosen to advertise my service by wearing a military hat, but I do wear my Veterans For Peace hat. I understand why others do, but a military hat is not for me. I can now talk about my service without regret, anger, or embarrassment. That is a huge step forward. The openness and forgiveness I experienced in Vietnam allowed me to weave a new tapestry, which I will carry for my remaining years.

Welcome Home!

The exclamation point to this trip came at the very end, returning to the San Francisco airport. As I exited the terminal, a 4' by 6' sign saying "WELCOME HOME, BUBBA" caught my attention. My first thought was: *That's strange. Another person with the same nickname as me. What are the chances? I wonder who this other guy is.* Then as I looked closer, the sign was being held by my two daughters, granddaughter, and grandson. The sign was for me! It was the WELCOME HOME that I never received on my first return from Vietnam. It was one of the momentous events of my life. I am beyond grateful for a family like this! The final gold thread completed my tapestry.

Energies
Sunny "Dos" Dosanjh

The Energy of Freedom is measured in time
Do you have the time to move as a whisper
Not caring about who hears you

Are you free
From mind and body
Or imprisoned, surrounded by
fire and brick walls

The Energy of Money is measured by food
Do bellies grumble from lack
Or groan from excess

Are you in a position to share
Or does hoarding
Becometh you

The Energy of Love is measured by light
The flame, the flicker
In darkness, does glow

And love eternal is visible
For those, who see it not
With only, their eyes.

Thank You For Your Service
G. Craige Edgerton

A young boy's fantasies,
Dreams of glory.
Built on the stories
Of World War II gory.

In the scrub and brush
Of his south Texas home,
He and his pals
The savannah they did roam.

Pretending to be Marines
They fought their way
Creating battles among the mesquite brush
And cactus decayed.

And he believed
The stories that were told.
The fantasies and revelry
Never got old.

It came to pass
When he exited school
His dreams of battle
Would begin to come true.

The hope of that war
Was just that.
A dream, lost and cynical
In the horror of combat.

An unknown land
Became known to all
As America's pride
Began to fall

Leaving the Corps
Disillusioned as hell
He hid his service
As under a turtle's shell.

Pride in the Corps
Was lost to the ages
As he buried three years
In his self-made cages.

"Who me a Marine?"
"Not a chance in hell"
Was the common refrain.
His story he would not tell.

Crying at movies
For reasons unknown.
Loud noises from nowhere
His reaction overblown.

Many years passed
As the SECRET remained hidden.
Reluctant to tell anyone.
That path was forbidden.

Like an apparition, that secret,
That haunted his every move.
Barely aware of it
But unable to remove.

After two score and ten years
He greeted the ghost.
He faced it head on
That dastardly host.

Facing this spook
Would test his mettle.
He decided it was time
To get this thing settled.

 But in the end
When all was said and done
When the curtain was dropped
And the phantom revealed.
The truth of his service
Was made clear one day
As he heard the store clerk:
"Thank you for your service"
Is all she had to say.

And he then understood.

Healing from Disappointment
Sunny "Dos" Dosanjh

The tree stood alone
Barren from the season of winter
The branches looked forlorn
The twigs brittle from frost

On occasion, a small bird would stop by
But it did not stay long

Time passed

Winter skies gave way to sunnier days
The morning dew came with its potion of elixir
And gradually as time moved forward
Life within the tree began anew

On occasion, a small bird would stop by
But now, it stayed and started to build a nest

Disappointment
Sunny "Dos" Dosanjh

Much was expected
Succeed I did
When failure hit once…it was an exception
When failure hit twice…ok, lesson wasn't learned

Now failure has hit 9 times, ten times and so on…
Even family, yells

Finally, I've learned that family doesn't always know
Finally, I've stopped listening to their negative dialogue
Finally, I've stopped

Now I move forward…with blessings towards family
Now I move forward…with forgiveness for family
Now I move forward.

Tomorrow is a new day
Birds will be singing
Grass and Trees will be smiling
And so will I

I'm not disappointed in myself anymore
Even though everyone around me is
I'll move forward
One moment at a time.

Home Again

Jaime Lee Johnson

On the road,
Searching everywhere.
A car speeds towards me,
Don't you dare.

In the mall,
Surrounded by noise.
Staring down children coming towards me,
Don't you dare.

A speedy exit,
Some semblance of safety found.
A man reaches into his jacket,
Don't you dare

Hair freshly cut,
Skin cool from a shave.
The plane lands in the desert,
Safe. I'm home again.

My Country
Doug Nelson

Ken Burns shook overripe peaches out of my tree. A soggy thump reminded me that when I came home from over there, people acted as if they didn't know me, and I think I no longer knew them.

I showed them slides of children by the roadside, and they said, "They're all just "communists," right?" or "They don't value human life the way we do."

As a child, a Nazi belt buckle I found in my father's army box said, "Gott Mit Uns", the words encircled in a wreath. Dad said, "God wasn't with them, was he?"

So, I had to wait fifty years to find out if he was with anybody before the elfin man and the nice lady behind the video mixer confirmed that my leaders had been unable to tell us, or even each other, why we were in Vietnam.

I don't know my country anymore. My country has exchanged the torch the lady in the harbor holds for an extended middle finger, and the orange clown is no longer funny. It is easy for me to love squealing toothless babies, my imperfect children who share my imperfections, my old friends, and this wife who loves me.

I love my country like the son of an abusive drunk who loves his father, like Lincoln's face on his Memorial, like ancient, twisted oaks on hillsides.

Two more generations after mine have been sent to war for reasons that make less and less sense. I love you, my country, but I cannot love what you keep doing, trying to be great (again), sending our sons and daughters to endless war.

Where Your Dreams Began
G. Craige Edgerton

A circle of men
Bearded, rounded, aged.
Some gracefully, most not.
A common bond binds them
Fifty years hence.

Young warriors
In a far-off land.
A stance against
Fallacious falling fragile
Dominoes… that weren't there.

The circle of men
Bare their souls.
Tell their stories.
Reveal their regrets.
Open their hearts.

And in that honesty,
In the bareing and telling and revealing and opening
They remember,
Where Their Dreams Began.

Dreams of glory, service, honor, and duty.
Dreams realized, and dreams shattered.
Dreams and nightmares indistinguishable.
Dreams recalled a lifetime later.

A young man's dreams

Are the old man's memories.
New dreams are created
Never too late to
Remember Where Your Dreams Began.

Abandoned No More
Sunny "Dos" Dosanjh

Words are empty and hollow
Their whisper is the only proof they existed
Now they are gone

What replaced them?
What could emerge from the silence?
New words emerged, heartfelt words,
words of sincerity words of healing,
words of inspiration, words of hope

I know not their origin
But I recognize their truth

Once they wove a tale of sorrow, of sadness
Grief, despair, loneliness and emptiness

Now the wheel has turned
Healing, hopeful and valued words
have taken their place

How did this happen?
Who shifted the wheel?
Why now?

And then it hit me
It's the same as Veterans in hospice
Nearing Death's door,
They put down their baggage
The stimulus is a fellow Veteran,

sitting by their side. It's a letting go
It's an unspoken word, unwritten word
But it is a moment that's understood
Without any words

I had been ready to leave
Life had lost its meaning, luster and allure
Love had left, Peace disappeared,
only pain remained

My life was broken
My sense of society's systems felt broken
I felt alone, was alone, and abandoned
to the words of torment
Better to die by the bottle
Than to live by words of gibberish

At the bottom, mercy arrived and smiled
I did not recognize her at first
But she walked with me in the food lines
She walked with me
As I walked the homeless path
And her presence was felt
As I lay on the floor each night
I had been ready to leave
But just like a Veteran in hospice
There was this…
This feeling, entity, spirit or understanding
So I called it mercy

I realized I was not alone
From moment to moment
The whispers from yesteryear
Formed words for me to hear

Get up, get up, get up
Soldier on, soldier on, soldier on Sunny Boy

I Yelled, I Exist! I'm NOT Expendable!
Can you help me?
Can you walk this path with me?

Stand by me one last time
With Honor and Remember
All Gave Some, Some Gave all

But I'm still here!
Get up, Get UP, GET UP!

Courage, Hope, Love
Faith, Truth, Honor
Dignity, Valor, Victorious

Now the words have life
Now they have meaning
Now the words smile at me
So I got up.

Liberation
Sunny "Dos" Dosanjh

I wish I knew what that meant.
The more help and therapy I seek
The more I feel disconnected

I'm learning the simple things
Sleep
Eat
Sleep
Eat.

Eat what?
I'm in the food bank line
With all the others who are hungry
I'm the lucky one.

No one cares about how smart or educated you are
No one cares about the trials & tribulations
that you've been through
They all have that same look of
"lost in the land of plenty"

One thing's for sure though
No one cares how you look … come as you are

No one cares about selling you anything or
wanting anything from you
Come as you are

It does feel like freedom

The line moves slowly along…it's been 2 hours
So I meditate and tell myself…
isn't liberation wonderful.

Reparations
Nick Butterfield

Could this place transcend time
when now has won.
This plane seems to be going fast
through the night and turbulence.
Enough so when we land we could
fix this thing.
With eyes shut wide open could once
again see
and someday fix this thing
that once was broken.

Welcome Home!
G. Craige Edgerton

It seems so trite
And overused.
"Thank you for your service".
The standard, rote salutation for
Those who serve.

The phrase now used for
Military, Nurses, Firefighters, Police and more
And deservedly so.
But what if Vietnam Veterans
Had their own greeting just for them?

Visiting Mt. Vernon,
Mr. Washington's home,
A wheelchair-bound
Veteran had a baseball cap
Announcing his Vietnam service.

I shook his hand,
Said I, too was there,
And he looked into my eyes
And replied:
"Welcome Home!"

Nothing more than
Two simple words.
A simple greeting for Vietnam Veterans
Long overdue.
"Welcome Home!"

Lost on the Path No More

Sunny "Dos" Dosanjh

I looked at the Devil and he smiled
I looked at God and he frowned
I looked at Mankind and was shunned

The Path headed to sorrow
The Path headed to despair
The Path headed to goodbye

From where, I don't know
From where, came a voice
From there, I was Lost on the Path No More

A Knotty Situation
G. Craige Edgerton

The first knot

As a kid, I occasionally went fishing with my dad. Although it was a somewhat fun activity, I always felt sorry for the fish, a poor little critter who'd been happily swimming around looking for something to eat, only to encounter a worm that, wham, suddenly began to fight back. The fish would flop around on the pier, struggling for air, while I wondered if a drowning person felt the same, desperately gulping lungfuls of water. Despite any real enthusiasm, I learned to tolerate fishing and, more importantly, learned a real-life lesson. Cast the damn bait properly, or you'll end up with a tangled mess in the reel…backlash!

My anger about Vietnam was similar to the backlash in a reel—a twisted jumble that seemed impossible to undo. Once the line got tangled into zillions of knots, I just wanted to throw the fishing tackle in the water, run away, and abandon it. I wanted to leave the mess where it was and never go fishing again. Problem solved, I thought. But the twisted line didn't go away, and neither did my anger about Vietnam. I buried it deep in my psyche, on the shelf behind my nightmares, hoping it would just disappear. Occasionally, I got glimpses of that hidden tangle in my mind. But I found it difficult to follow the line and undo the knots.

During our fishing trips, my dad made me undo the backlash. He patiently showed me how to untangle the line and prevent the problem from happening again. He taught me to look closely at the knot, find the entry and exit points, go from there, and work on the binds one-by-one. A backlash couldn't be untangled all at once. When I got frustrated and lost control, I asked my Dad for help. Eventually, with his guidance, I focused my attention and probed carefully with my fingers until I found the keystone knot—the one knot that, when loosened, freed the entire mess.

Why didn't I just untie that big keystone anger knot back in 1971 when I left the Marine Corps? Why did it take 50 years to slowly, painstakingly identify the smaller knots that eventually led back to the mother of all knots?

Before going to the Veterans Administration (VA) for help, I dipped my toes in the water and made a first attempt. I participated in a 5-year study focused on the relationship between PTSD, sleep apnea, and memory loss at the VA in Palo Alto, CA. I'd experienced none of the symptoms described in the study and, unfortunately, never found out if I was part of the control group, as it was a confidential study. Nevertheless, I came to my own conclusions. I knew I had mild sleep apnea and memory loss, but I definitely did not have PTSD!

At that time, I didn't know anything about the depths of my anger or PTSD. Just as I'd looked to my dad for help with the fishing line, I needed help from someone who understood my anger about the war and how it affected me. When I took the critical step of reaching out to the Vet Center, a part of the VA, I began to untangle my disordered feelings and beliefs about Vietnam.

The Second Knot

Once I accepted the fact that I still had issues regarding Vietnam, the first knot, I resolved to deal with them. It was time to find and untie the second knot, which was a little more complicated than the first. Pick here; pull there. Find what is connected to what. Look at the big picture, then zoom in on the detail. However, I was constantly frustrated, unable to find the source of the tangle. Confusion overwhelmed me. My counselor, who had helped many veterans with similar problems, gently guided me to untangle the knot for myself, just like my dad had done.

The thought that "they" made me do it had a vice grip on my

mind. "They" made me violate my personal moral code dedicated to protecting the little guy from the bogeyman and what I thought was the Marine Corps code of protecting Americans.

This moral injury was the deepest knot, leading me to spend a lifetime trying to justify my combat experience in Vietnam. I had been raised with a strong Catholic faith and took seriously the golden rule and some of the teachings of the Ten Commandments. I had stopped being a practicing Catholic soon after leaving home to go to St. Edwards University, but I retained certain basic beliefs about right and wrong. Vietnam blew much of that apart. An old saying from World War II, "There are no atheists in a foxhole," I changed to "There are only atheists in a foxhole." I thought how anybody could believe in a god with all this destruction and man's inhumanity to his fellow man.

After experiencing combat, I couldn't believe that god would create beings that were capable of such hatred and destruction. Some might reply to this that it is not god who created this horrible behavior but the devil. That then brings the question, who created the devil? God, of course, because according to those who believe in god, he created all things. I always hoped that someone, someday, could explain god to me without resorting to "take it on faith," "because I believe it," or "it's in the bible". All people have a "story" they believe in to guide them through life, and for those who accept god, I was okay with that as long as they did not try to make me believe it. If someone asked me to prove gravity, I could drop a 10-pound weight on their foot. There—proof! My belief, or "story", was founded in science and nature and didn't rely on "faith" to be true.

From the beginning of my therapy, I questioned myself again and again. *Why can't I just let it go?* Why couldn't I accept that mistakes were made all around and everyone involved had the best intentions at the time? It was over and done with, and nothing could un-ring that bell. Forgive and forget. It seemed so easy to say but extremely difficult to untangle the mental knots that held me in their grip.

"Were you a good Marine while in Vietnam?" asked my therapist on one June day in 2019.

"Huh?" I responded quizzically. I didn't understand the question.

"What do you mean?"

"Did you do what you were told and perform your duties as expected as a Marine officer? Did you shirk your duty or do your best, regardless of the circumstances?"

"Of course, I did what was expected of me, and I did it to the best of my ability," I said. "While in Vietnam, I didn't question my duties and performed admirably. I was promoted to First Lieutenant while there."

"Are you able to separate your individual service from your opinions about the government and how it screwed things up? Can you see that there are two different trains of thought here?" the therapist asked.

I sat puzzled as my mind began to shift. It was a slight movement, but with it, my whole perspective on my experience of Vietnam began to change.

Wham! The source of the knot! Gently, I began to tug and untangle. The knot began to unwind as I separated my service from what I felt about the war. The idea seeped into my awareness, gently at first, then like a thunderbolt. *I was not the war*. I was a small cog in a massive wheel. For 47 years, I had passionately believed that *I was the war*, that my participation de facto made me so. But this simple question, "Craige, were you a good Marine?" allowed me to separate the two and continue reconciling with myself. The knots were loosening.

"So, can you see the difference between these two thoughts, Craige?" my counselor reiterated.

My mind was swirling. I could barely focus on what he was saying. My emotions and beliefs about my time in Viet Nam were being turned upside down.

"I think I can. I can see what you are saying, but it's still unclear.

I'll think about it over the next few weeks...But does this mean I must wear the hat?" I asked sarcastically.

For months, my counselor suggested I wear a Vietnam veteran hat. He also encouraged me to say the Pledge of Allegiance out loud or sing a patriotic song at my weekly Kiwanis meeting. For over 35 years, I had refused to do any of this as a form of silent protest about my time in Vietnam. I had become so attached to my anger that it had become like an arm or leg to me. To lose my rage would be like losing a limb. I might change my mind about the war, but there was no way I was wearing that freaking hat!

The counselor's suggestion that I separate my military service from the irrationality of the war began to unfold slowly in my mind, like dawn on a clear summer day—imperceptibly at first, then growing brighter and brighter. He had also suggested that I walk in the Veterans Day Parade in San Jose, California, as a way to accept the public's appreciation. I tried that once but never again. *"Those folks in the parade were honoring me, not the war,"* he thought. *"So how do I let go of this belief I have held close for so long?"*

The Third Knot

A nasty backlash doesn't give up easily. Two knots down...how many more to go? All I could do was dig deeper until I got them all.

Since returning from Vietnam, I assumed my anger was unique among my fellow veterans. Seeing so many others wearing their Vietnam veteran hats, I was sure all the other Marines returned proud of their service. That is until I started attending group therapy sessions at the Vet Center.

Group therapy sessions were part of the process from the beginning with my counselor. The group sessions allowed me to talk one-on-one with other Vietnam vets and hear their stories. Stories of drugs, alcohol, difficulty holding jobs, holding too many jobs, overwork, divorce, isolation, inability to maintain good relationships with children, sleeplessness, nightmares, hair-trigger reactions to loud noises, flashing lights, and crowds were a part of everyone's story. It was as if I was talking to myself in a mirror. I saw that anger was widespread in the Vet Center group, although it was, as I saw in myself, as well camouflaged as a rifleman preparing for an ambush. I finally realized that I was not alone in my feelings and that many vets had repressed their rage for just as long, if not longer, than me.

I began to understand that connecting with others was healing, a big life lesson for me. Knowing that my experiences, especially the negative ones, were not unique and that I was not alone in being pissed off for so long was an enlightening moment. Somehow, sharing the anger lessened its hold and allowed me to start the undoing process. I felt consoled, and another knot began to be untangled.

Through the support of the Vet Center group, I could pull back the curtain and begin to discover why I felt so angry. I finally saw that I had fabricated a story from somewhat nebulous facts. Were LBJ and McNamara truly evil with nefarious intentions? Was the falling domino theory really a ruse? Or did they sincerely believe it? Those were unanswerable questions, but they opened up new possibilities. I could now reimagine that narrative just as I had created a particular story about my war experience. Just hearing the stories of the other veterans and realizing that I was not alone in my being pissed off had loosened the third knot. The question then became: are there more knots? Only time will tell.

A New Perspective: Releasing the Knot

In the early 90s, a revelation came to me in a deep meditation with a group of other men seeking their place in life. I was traveling along a path in meditation when I encountered a log. I couldn't go around, over, under, or through it. I was stuck as the log blocked all movement forward. As I tried to figure out how to get past it, it gradually began to take the shape of a door. I gazed at the door for a while before it dawned on me: *Open* it!

Slowly, I approached the door and tested it to see if it was locked. It wasn't, so I gently turned the doorknob, and it swung open. On the other side, I saw that the path continued without further obstructions, so I proceeded with my meditative journey, forgetting about the log.

I have recalled this meditation session, on and off, over the years. At the time, I shared my psychic journey with the meditation group, and they presented me with an interpretation of my story: *The block is the opening*.

"The block is the opening"? I thought at the time. "That doesn't make any sense. They are contradictory. They are opposites. How can opposites be equal"?

I wasn't about to be fooled. My favorite class at St. Edwards University was logic. Syllogisms were used to assess a statement or premise and prove it "logical" or "illogical." Black or white, with no gray in between. Logic was my way to make sense of the world throughout my life. It was how I determined what was right and what was wrong. It was clear to me that opposites could not be equal. It would be illogical, against reason. It just couldn't be!

So much for logic; it usually works, but not in all cases, as I learned after many years of life experience. I eventually understood from "The Block is the Opening" that **challenges along life's path can also be opportunities.** I could see the block as an obstacle that couldn't be overcome, or I could choose to see the door as an "opening." The point of view I chose made all the difference.

With that same group of men from the meditation, I studied Carlos Castaneda, a shaman in the Toltec tradition, who taught that individuals observe the world through their own personal "assemblage points." Our thoughts, feelings, emotions, and beliefs about ourselves and the world around us are like a series of energetic lines emanating from our consciousness to the outer world. Castaneda felt that these energetic lines created our outer world. By slightly shifting our assemblage point, where the lines come together in our mind, we could shift how we see the world. Simply changing a thought could generate a critical shift in perspective. My assemblage point was shifting, and with it, my emotions and beliefs about Vietnam.

From these experiences, the meditation, the assemblage point, and help from my counselor, I began to modify my understanding of my war experience. I was able to shift my assemblage point by shifting my thoughts. "You are the war," the block, became "You are not the war," the opening, creating a completely new perspective. **One little word, "not," released the "knot" and changed my life!**

Does this mean I am ready to walk proudly in a Veteran's Day Parade? Probably not. I will be content to accept that *I was not the war*. I was a participant *in the war*, but not the war itself. I can live with that. No, I can't un-ring that devastating bell, but I can choose to hear that chime as a sweet melody rather than a harsh call to anger.

My story does not have an ending…so far. My story, once buried, is now an open, ongoing dialogue with myself and those close to me. Avoidance was appropriate when the pain, hurt, embarrassment, and anger were too much to bear on my own. I have abandoned that strategy and followed a healing path by sharing my story with others. With the help of my wife, Jan, my family, especially my daughters Karen and Elizabeth, the Vet Center, my counselor, and my fellow compatriot Veterans, I am now able to connect with that young boy in South Texas who always wanted to be a Marine and can now walk with a little more pride in his step.

But it's doubtful I will ever wear that freaking Vietnam veteran's hat!

A Thread I Follow

Jim Marney-Petix

There's a thread I follow,

It is kindness.

At times, my duty has been the opposite,

I have been a monster.

The memories don't go away.

The thread doesn't go away.

I judge myself.

I feel broken.

I will heal, as we all must.

Will I live to see it?

Don't Say Goodbye to Nobody
Nick Butterfield

These days I see my reflection in water and sometimes
save bees from drowning.
Bees that thought
water was air and breathed.
I remember tropical leaves that appeared to have
no branches burned into our DNA forever and bombs
left unexploded.
I believe that in Vietnam there is still hope. Hope
where blue sky appears through the canopy of jungle,
where tigers and elephants once lived.
I believe in
dreams where air is freedom and we are ghosts
somewhere in the middle.
I believe the past
and the future points to a mountain peak above the clouds.
What is left behind, only a vision,
the ripples we still feel when we say good-
b
y
e

I Am Home
Sunny "Dos" Dosanjh

He lay there taking his last few breaths
The little mouse was fighting for his life
I found the little mouse
In front of the refrigerator
He was unable to move

I placed a plastic bag in front of him
Cut up a piece of sweet potato
And placed it in front of him
He barely moved but took two more steps

Gently,
I nudged him into the plastic bag
And we went for a walk to the corner park

In the middle,
Where the sun hits the brightest
I found a squirrel hole

I undid the knot on the plastic bag
And gently rolled him out
Into the squirrel hole

The hole was of perfect length
His head now lay on the dirt
Eyes were fading off into the mystic
His heart was fighting for his life

I placed the few bits

Of sweet potato around him
Covered him with some twigs and leaves
Leaving enough room for air and light
And knelt down beside him

Then the memory hit me…

Over a decade ago, I was an inmate
for several months at the
County Jail in Milpitas, California
We, inmates, used to save the peanuts
From the chow hall
And feed them to the squirrels
They were inmates also but they acted free

One particular squirrel
Had lost the use of its hind legs
We called him Stumpy
Stumpy would crawl towards all of us
He was not afraid

Whichever inmate was closest
would feed Stumpy
And Stumpy grew into the fattest squirrel
He became family
There wasn't too much else
That we inmates could do
But we always talked about Stumpy
He was loved

BOOM
It was early Sunday morning
BOOM
Holy shit!

I Am Home

BOOM, BOOM, BOOM, BOOM, BOOM

Startled, I got up from the lower bunk
And ran outside to take stock
I was not expecting that sight

An exterminator was doing his job
Lowered his cannon type of contraption
And blew his ordinance
into each squirrel hole
BOOM, BOOM, BOOM, BOOM, BOOM

I turned around
Walked back to the bunk
And just sat there

That afternoon, after chow
The inmates gathered as we usually did
With our peanuts
It was silent…

Now
I knelt down by this dying little mouse
On my phone, a Sikh Kirtan,
holy poem was playing

Now
As an American Legion Chaplain for the
San Francisco Bay Area & Monterey Bay
As Captain of the American Legion Honor Guard,
District 13, Santa Clara County, Silicon Valley
As the Service Officer for the
American Legion Post 419 Santa Clara
I knelt

I said the prayer from my Christian upbringing
Our Father, Who Art In Heaven
Hallowed Be Thy Name…

I sang the sacred song from my Catholic teachings
 as a young boy
Gaudēte, gaudēte!
Chrīstus est nātus
Ex Marīā virgine,
gaudēte!…

I sang the prayer of my Mother and Father
from my Sikh upbringing
Ik Onkar, Satnam, Karta Purakh…

I said the prayer verse of my Muslim friends
Allah O Akbar…

I said the prayer verse of my Hindu friends
Om Nama Shiva…

I said the prayer verse of my Jewish friends
Shema Yisrael, Adonai Eloheinu, Adonai Echad…

I held onto my meditative thoughts of love
As Buddhist Monks, Toltecs, Shamans
and Mystics were apt to do…

The Past was over
Life in the Present was over for the little mouse

As the Cold of Winter struck his home
And the last leaf fell from his tree

My heart, my soul, my spirit, my everlasting
Prayed for the little mouse
Prayed for Stumpy and his friends
Prayed for All Souls who had gone before…

May they All realize warmth, blessing, love
May they All realize your light of divinity
May they All realize that they are Home

And for your humble servant
May your words of Faith awaken me to say,
"No longer shall I wander"
"No longer am I lost"
Truly it is an Amazing Grace that says
 "I once was lost, but Now I'm found"

I'm no longer blind
I choose Heaven Here On Earth
I fought the Devil and bear the scars
Sacrifice I did, my Angelic Wing

As did many a GI
Welcome Home! To all All Warriors
Who live to tell their tale
We Are Home! So enjoy the Spring,
Summer and Fall
And together we shall smile,
Sing and laugh for finally,
I am Home!

Haiku Vietnam
Nick Butterfield

(Upon arriving at a blind center that makes incense sticks, 2024)

The roof is leaking
But it's us that cannot see
Monsoon rains begins

Once enemies
Both wore sandals when they met
Autumn moon setting

Hoa Lo Prison
An opened Christmas package
Sent by U.S. mail

Surely You Know Private Nelson
Doug Nelson

The young soldier came home from the war safely and gratefully. So many friends and others he didn't know could not. So the general is on the news, a four-star, who tells us in his words that Afghanistan was hopelessly mismanaged, that our country farmed out too many functions to contractors, this old guy with a massive plaque of ribbons to show that he had been in wars his entire adult life.

Recently, a civilian controlling a drone from his desk, guided by intelligence reports and lawful orders, had killed ten Afghan civilians in their family car. The generals had said that only terrorists were killed. But then, they called it a mistake when the facts came out.

The soldier's dad remembered a veteran speaking for peace, who later ran for president, who said, fifty years ago, asking what soldier or marine wants to be the last to die for a mistake? Mismanaged? We didn't mean to kill children?

Where does that leave us, the soldier, one veteran among millions of others who did our missions as best we could, who won some and lost some, and who took care of each other because it was all we could do?

The US Secretary of Defense was interviewed while driving his car in Washington, D.C., on Constitution Avenue, and said to a reporter that he and the rest of the suits knew that the Vietnam War could not be won, suggesting that my buddies and I should not have been there.

In Vietnam, I was troubled after hearing a conversation among soldiers in line at the post office, saying that they had discovered a North Vietnamese rear supply and hospital area and had captured what appeared to be nurses because they had the smooth, unblemished hands of educated women The guy said, "We did 'em, then we shot 'em". I shared what I had heard with my commanding officer, catching him in a rare moment of rest at his desk. After a pause, the major said, "Private Nelson, surely you know that shitty things happen in war". I was advised not to spread hearsay information I had no way to prove. I took his advice.

Shitty things happen, not the least of which is going to war for the wrong reasons or for no reason.

Paying It Forward
Jaime Lee Johnson

Teaching is something that I had no idea I would enjoy doing. I don't mean in the school classroom with students, though I have done it in a similar environment. But in either one on one or in a group setting, it allows me to pass on knowledge I have gathered over the years. Sometimes through simple experimentation or trial and error. Sometimes through sweat, blood, and tears. Be it from a hard working job or the pains and the absolute chaos of combat.

Lessons hard learned that can be of great importance to someone struggling with real issues, but unsure of how to deal with them. A friend struggling with depression, a coworker not sure how to organize a task before completing it, or someone at an impasse regarding a crafting project. If I know something about it, I'm almost too eager to help. It has sometimes gotten me in trouble in the sense of appearing arrogant, but what else am I supposed to do? Just stand there and let things go wrong? Not if I can do something about it. I always offer help. Especially to those whom I call a friend.

I have personally received such help when I felt there was nothing I could do and I have not just a need, but a duty to pass that on.

The Light of Fire
Sunny "Dos" Dosanjh

Winter had arrived
She pierced me

I did not know
How cold Winter could be
Now I know

Winter said Summer had died
He had Fallen

For Death came knocking at his door
He answered.
Now he is gone

Winter is here in front of you…
My Son is gone
Who are you?

I looked into her eyes
Tears were forming
Vowing to stand firm

And then I looked into her Soul
Kindled I did the Sacred
Light the fire I did
And the tears fell

Winter gave way to Spring.

The Magical Room
G. Craige Edgerton

An ordinary room.
No artwork. Bright fluorescent lights.
Tables in a rectangle,
Thirty-five men gather.

Aging, most in their late 70s.
Many wearing hats
Emblazoned with their unit
A calling card for their proud service.

But in this ordinary room
Magic is created.
Veterans, not all from Vietnam,
Reunite to tell their stories.

From a place of avoidance,
Isolation, embarrassment, and anger,
Or from proud service, patriotism,
Gratitude and honor. They gather.

Souls are bared.
Stories and lies are recalled.
Laughter and tears merge.
Hearts open…in this ordinary room.

In this ordinary room
The magic is a brotherhood
Remembered and recreated
A new, old family.

Talking, listening, respect,
Sharing, discovering and
So much more.
Transform this ordinary room
Into a MAGICAL ROOM.

I AM. I WAS.

G. Craige Edgerton

I AM the war,
Absorbed into my being,
Who am I,
A measure of my essence.
An anchor dragging me down.

I WAS IN the war,
The storm reduced
To a gentle breeze.
An anchor cut loose.
I can breathe again.

A tiny shift
I AM to I WAS IN
Changes my world.
Releases me.
Peace at last.

An Internal War
G. Craige Edgerton

Over time, I learned to live with my hidden nightmare. By 2015, I had established myself in the Valley of Heart's Delight in San Jose, California, where I raised two daughters, married a second time, worked in various careers, and became a leader in the local environmental community and a volunteer in many service projects over the course of four decades.

The horrors and shame of Vietnam remained buried in my memory, far away from day-to-day life. I thought that if I refused to focus on them, the bad memories would disappear. But they didn't. They festered inside, mostly forgotten. A nasty little voice, barely perceptible, seeped around the edges of my mind. Many years later, triggered by unexpected events, it was time for me to let that little voice start to speak to me.

In 1991, my wife Jan and I were at the movie *For The Boys* with Bette Midler as a USO performer who entertained troops in World War II, Korea, and Vietnam. At one point, the scene was an artillery firebase in Vietnam—exactly like the ones I had been stationed at. Suddenly, I started crying uncontrollably and was immediately transported back to FB Neville. All the regret, embarrassment, disgust, and anger at the war and the Marine Corps poured out of that hidden place in my mind, spilling into my consciousness.

"What the hell is going on?" I asked Jan. "I've never had this kind of reaction to a movie and have no idea what was festering inside me."

It was the moment when I realized something was not quite right—with me or my relationship to the Vietnam War. I wished Vietnam had stayed buried in my cemetery of bad memories, but the movie had released something that could not be put back.

It wasn't just the movie that impacted me, though. On a bright summer day in the early 2000s, I was at a business meeting in an outdoor restaurant when a low-flying jet roared over, seemingly out of nowhere. I dropped to my knees and covered my head, my body quaking. The other meeting participants barely registered the jet and were startled to see me fall to the ground. Incredibly embarrassed, I sensed again that something was not quite right.

And then, around that same time, while shopping in Costco, I was maneuvering around a Costco employee operating a small forklift, restocking shelves. Suddenly, a loud BANG rang out as the worker accidentally dropped an empty wooden pallet that fell flat on the concrete floor just a few feet away. I grabbed my ears and dropped to the floor, shaking. I crouched behind the shopping cart for what felt like a full minute, though it may only have been seconds. Luckily, my wife, Jan, was there to help calm me. All the other shoppers barely noticed it. My first reaction was anger at myself and embarrassment at having made such a scene. My reaction had an eerie rhyme with his previous movie experience.

I was embarrassed and puzzled by my reactions to these sudden loud noises and other triggers. Why did I react so differently to these minor disturbances while others easily shook them off? Was it in my DNA? Was I just a little different and unusually sensitive to loud, sudden noises?

A few years later, Jan and I went to see another movie, "The Fog of War," a 2003 documentary about Robert McNamara, LBJ's secretary of defense during the Vietnam War. In the film, McNamara confessed that the Johnson administration knew they couldn't win the war but refused to admit it. They didn't want to be in charge during the first war that the U.S. lost. I was shocked and furious at McNamara's admission. Why I hadn't responded to this information with the same kind of outrage years earlier when I first heard it, I couldn't explain. It wasn't until much later that I understood how deep my avoidance and denial of the war was.

I rarely spoke of my time in the Marine Corps or Vietnam with Jan, so she had no idea I was carrying such anger. And neither did

I. These separate events brought my anger to a boiling point, but I still didn't know what to do about it. I realized I had an opportunity to deal with my tangled feelings head-on but didn't yet have the mechanism or the guts to try. The solution came from the Veterans Administration (VA), which I had avoided since leaving the Marine Corps.

In May 2015, an old Marine Corps buddy visited me. He was a longtime gung-ho Marine still living in rural Texas, who persuaded me to seek help from the VA. He had been in Vietnam but not in combat. He was receiving disability for Parkinson's Disease, which was attributable to his exposure to Agent Orange. Another friend and veteran later chimed in with a similar suggestion. With their encouragement, I started to look into the VA for help. By this time, after my multiple unexplained reactions, I realized something wasn't quite right with me, and I was ready to explore at least getting help from the VA.

It took me a few weeks to consider it. It was difficult to accept aid from the military establishment, which I had loathed for so long. The possibility of digging up long-buried memories after 47 years of avoidance was, at a minimum, scary and, at worst, could be devastating.

Ultimately, I decided it might be good to check out the VA. After all, they offered free medical care and other support, and it was in my blood to never turn down "free." I finally took the plunge and scheduled my first appointment with a VA medical doctor in August 2015.

At my first physical checkup appointment, Dr. Stetz asked me routine medical questions and about my military service.

"Were you in Vietnam? Yes. Did you see combat? Yes. What service were you in? The Marine Corps," I answered. He suspected I had been in Vietnam because of my age.

"Have you been tested for PTSD?" asked Dr. Stetz.

"No, I don't have PTSD," I said.

The doctor persisted and began listing off the various symptoms of PTSD. The dimmer switch in my brain started to increase slowly, letting the light gradually brighten. Things I had experienced but could never explain started to become clearer. Though I resisted the diagnosis of PTSD, Dr. Stetz convinced me to at least talk to the Vet Center, a VA organization helping veterans with issues involving combat, mostly PTSD. Reluctantly, I agreed to go just one time to put the PTSD issue to rest. *What the hell am I getting into?* I thought as I pondered the possibilities.

The Vet Center was housed in a small office on North First Street in San Jose, crammed with outdated furniture, tables piled with various service magazines, and patriotic posters featuring flags, guns, and young men and women with determination in their eyes. Hours-old coffee and stale donuts sat on the side table.

My first meeting at the Vet Center was a bit disturbing. The counselor asked me some initial questions about my age, marital status, family, work experience, hobbies, etc. About halfway through the appointment, some gentle but pointed questions came up about my experience in Vietnam. He explained that they would not delve into those experiences right then but invited me to come back for a second meeting to begin that more difficult conversation.

I resisted the idea of going back. I felt that he should be spending time with Vets who really needed help instead of someone like me, who'd led a rather ordinary but successful life after my wartime service. And yet, in that first conversation, he had opened a door, and I sensed, deep down, that important and disturbing parts of myself were hidden behind that door.

It was time to open it and face my future.

Dumpster Diving

G. Craige Edgerton

Evidence can incriminate.
When evidence is gone, the crime is gone.
My Marine Corps uniform
Was the condemning evidence.

A dumpster is now home
To the icon of my Marine Corps time.
The evidence now destroyed.
I never served.

So too, monochrome grainy photos,
Hidden, hopefully, lost forever.
A reminder of Vietnam,
Resurface 17 years later.
Destined for a second dumpster.

The wisdom and love
Of my prescient 14-year-old daughter
Intercepts the photos dumpster run.
She keeps them hidden, waiting for me.

The reunion happens
Thirty years later.
When I'm ready.
When I began to heal.

The photos, now valuable,
A window to proud service.
Avoidance becomes acceptance.
Trash turned to Treasure.

Remnants of A Past Life

Jaime Lee Johnson

Pain. Every morning. Pain. It wakes me when it wants to, not when I want to. It disturbs my mind and causes me to lash out at those undeserving of my anger, while it also reminds me of what once was and will never be again. The dull ache rages through my body as I struggle to sit up and on the edge of me bed, my back slouched as I attempt to straighten that which has awoken me from what slumber I fought to obtain during the night. Only for a few moments, but it's as if I sit there, motionless, for what feels like an age before I can muster the strength to stand and get on with what lies before me in my day.

Walking now. To what, I'm not really sure. My mind has yet to recover from the battle I just fought, so I stumble and wander about my apartment until an idea breaks through the cobwebs still wrapped around it.

Not every morning is like this, but it does happen often enough to take notice. Sometimes it's a battle of wills. The will to stay, to return to my bed and allow the pain to win. Or the will to fight, to push through it all and see my brothers once more in a support group meeting or at an event. Men who have fought and suffered infinitely more than I have or ever will. So the battle rages on, in both my mind and my body, to see the day through to its end.

Even on the worst day, it eventually proves fruitful and filled with the joy of even the slightest accomplishment. I ride that feeling of victory and use it to guide my mind to a better future for myself. One where the pain still exists, but it no longer clouds my judgment or keeps me from enjoying what little I have left after years of service and sacrifice.

Yellow Palace

G. Craige Edgerton

Tattered and torn;
She, draped in yellow,
Pocked with bullet holes.
A casualty of war.

First seen in 1969,
Passing by in my GI jeep.
The grand dame,
A long-held, vivid memory.

French Colonial
Two stories tall
A tale of history
Shattered in Hue, Vietnam.

Fifty-five years later
She is fully restored
I encounter her grandeur
Stately, along the Perfume River.

She from destitution
To splendor.
Me from Guilt
To Forgiveness.

Military Veteran Dog Tags
Sunny "Dos" Dosanjh

It's 69 degrees on a beautiful, blue sky, sunny day. There's a slight breeze which makes the leaves rustle ever so quietly. I could be anywhere, but I'm here. What I didn't know was that I was still at war.

My Dog Tags, once worn on Active-Duty, are now worn on a lost, confused Veteran. I'm older now and it's become an automatic action of wearing my dog tags everywhere I go. Worn visibly on top of any shirt. I don't know why but I need to change a few mind sets but I didn't realize I needed to start with my own mind.

A few years back, I had gotten into a bad car accident. I remember the paramedics ripping my clothes off of me and I didn't care to survive. However, I did. Someone took my belongings, along with my blood-soaked clothes and dog tags, then dropped them off at my parents house.

They thought I had died.

Time passed. But I had not.

I once mentioned that I was lost and confused to a person who was not in a position to help. He asked, "why are you confused?" It was my mistake to ask a civilian about a Military Veterans mindset. He just looked at me with disdain, disappointment and lack of respect. Note to self, stay clear of civilians. Thus the self-isolation and the downward spiral into alcoholism. These civilians are everywhere…I don't trust them.

My mental war had taken it's toll. I couldn't see it but it was clear that I was still fighting an imagined war. The price of this mental war was high. It cost me everything. The same day my ex-wife asked for a divorce, I went to work and got laid off. Within one hour, my world was turned upside down…how could this not be a war against forces that I cannot see. I thought that I had hit rock bottom,

I had not.

Several years later, I became jobless, homeless and penniless. Prison system was calling my name, IRS was auditing me, court systems wanted alimony & child support, every credit card maxed out, car in repossession, kids not talking to me, couldn't pass a background check due to court case, no money so borrowing from family and ended up on food stamps. I was in the middle of a mental war and I was losing the will to fight, to live or survive. I didn't care, I let go…

Letting go is liberating. I don't care if I survive the day…I don't care about love, family, friends, money, sex, cars, sports, homes, food, drink or a god I didn't understand. So the mental war raged on.

My mind saw the enemy everywhere, they come at me in the dark but they set me up during the day. Be wary of those civilians who smile and be cautious of anyone in a Military or Veterans role was my daily mindset. They tried to kill me during Active-Duty, but I survived. I've never trusted anyone in uniform since. How could I trust anyone in the civilian world that didn't even understand the military mindset so where could I go…I was lost, and confused, and the old stoic motto of "suck it up" didn't work for me. I was capable of hurting others, so I needed to disappear from society.

It's now 70 degrees. The sun is easing its way into my soul. It whispers to my heart about a young boy who once lived unafraid. There was an honor in being unafraid, fearless, and courageous. Now it appears that there is no honor in letting go or giving up on life before it has run its course. So I try to learn how to die a dignified death…perhaps like a Warrior, but with no rank, military branch or physical war…just a lost and confused warrior fighting a mental, imagined war.

Up to this point, I didn't have belief or faith in anything. All that started to slowly change as I "let go"

What more did I have but my breath. But then I realized I could exercise a bit and due to my status of poverty, I was lucky to have water, soup and vegetables on a daily basis. I obtained this at a Sikh Gurdwara (Temple) which provided free, hot meals every day. So exercise and having both a spiritual and food diet became my norm.

That's when the light within became lit.

Not only with Sikhism but Christianity, Hinduism, Buddhism, Judaism, Islam and many other non-religious but spiritual practices. The divine had entered into my mind, heart and soul. Grace had made it's presence felt and the Almighty took me aside to observe my thoughts about the imagined, mental war.

At the same time, a fellow American Legionnaire was walking by me and noticing my dog tags nonchalantly asked, "Why you still at War?" He just kept on walking and at the time, I didn't think anything of it.

In our Veterans book club, a Vietnam Veteran commented about "I am the War" versus "I was in War" and just like that…dots connected. I now had the ability to observe the thoughts, saw that it was all imagined, and just like that, my mentality switched.

I put away the dog tags.

My imagined mental war with everyone was over. The hatred, anger, resentment and those feelings of anxiety, depression and suicide over the course of 35 years had subsided. An inner peace had arrived, calmness of spirit and a newfound joy of being alive for one more day.

It's now 71 degrees, however, it feels like I'm in heaven. The sun is softly warming me and I feel like I'm being embraced by the entire universe. I'm no longer alone, "The God" that is without is also "The God" within. For me, it's nameless, shapeless, formless, does nothing but leaves nothing undone.

Today, I wear two dog tags, one with my name and the other "anonymous" for I did not know which one would make it back. As of today, I'm transforming them from a symbol of war into a symbol for a Spiritual Warrior of Peace.

Kintsugi Haiku

Bill Noyes

Life's broken pieces
With golden wishes bound
Glitter bright again.

Shattered shards pressed
Together are golden parts
Building wisdom's dream.

Judgment
Jaime Lee Johnson

Everyone seeks a place where they can feel safe.

A place where they can breathe.

A place where those around them understand how they feel
and what they have and are going through.

What generation they're from or where they grew up
has no bearing on what those men have gone through.

It's a place where a man can be with his brothers
and feel loved.

It's a place where when I am struggling,
I know there is someone that will help me up.

And most importantly, it is a place I will not feel judged.

His Name Is On The Wall
G. Craige Edgerton

It stands, unadorned, alone, black, polished.
A stark reminder
Of America's first lost war.
58,320 names carved in black granite.
His name is on the Wall.

He left on patrol that day.
Thirty comrades and him.
Six returned, twenty five not.
They came home in body bags.
Their names are on the Wall.

He took my place on the chopper.
Where I should have been.
It was 3 days shy of his 20th birthday.
He never met his daughter.
His name is on the Wall.

They trained together,
Becoming brothers.
Shipped out as one, fought as one.
But not all came home as one.
More names on the Wall.

My next door neighbor.
The first from my hometown.
He helped me drag
Bodies to the chopper.
His name is on the Wall.

We all know someone on the Wall.
All of us who fought there.
And we are all so thankful,
Oh, so thankful.
That our names are not on the Wall.

It Happened Unexpectedly
G. Craige Edgerton

The unexpected happened while I waited for Kamala to give her acceptance speech at the DNC in August 2024. The unexpected was me buying into the show of PATRIOTISM. Good old-fashioned, flag-waving, singing, balloon-dropping, and RAH-RAH for the United States of America. It is syrupy, loud, colorful, and unabashed by every slice of the people who make up this unique American pie.

Why was patriotism unexpected? I grew up in conservative south Texas and attended too many years of Catholic schools and catechism, even graduating from a Catholic university. Upon graduation, I joined the Marine Corps and saw combat in Vietnam as a Marine assigned to an infantry company. If anyone should have been patriotic, it was me. But I have avoided and abhorred this flag-waving, America right or wrong, patriotism since before I ever left the Marines.

To me, patriotism, America right or wrong patriotism, seemed always to be tied to the military. Jets flying in formation, gun salutes, parades with soldiers preceded by the American Flag, and fireworks all gave honor and glory to a filthy business, the business of killing as many people as quickly and as efficiently as possible.

So, why was I seduced into the patriotism at the DNC, a patriotism that I so despised? It was the fresh air. It was the lifting of a heavy weight off my shoulders. It was sanity, hope, and even the possibility of freedom that I grew up with that was familiar to me. Somehow, the patriotism of that event felt different than it should be like it was "back in the day."

But then reality struck. As the days ticked away after the DNC, the sugar high receded. I returned to my previous reality as I interacted with various Veterans who still believed that being in war was an honorable calling. And I can understand if the calling is that: honorable. For many Vietnam veterans, Gulf War veterans, or any Veteran with trauma, the calling was not always honorable. Although the service was honorable, the reasons for being there were not. Wars with no clear enemy, dubious goals, lies piled on top of lies, and disastrous outcomes are not a calling.

I look forward to a future patriotic parade with bands, prancing horses, teachers, immigrants and native-born, police and firefighters, and all those who stand up for and protect the little guy. Now, that's a patriotic parade that I would not only gladly attend but, be proud to participate in.

Common Ground
Sunny "Dos" Dosanjh

The word *"Grounded"* appears to have a few negative connotations associated with it

I think of a flight *grounded*
I think of a career *grounded*
I think of a life *grounded*

However,
This morning, I sat with my bare feet resting on the grass and soil...
And I felt, *grounded*.

Life's circumstances can ground a person in a negative way...
But it can also do the opposite.

Grounded in Faith
Grounded by Nature
Grounded with Gratitude

So, I ask myself...despite the journey I've been on...

Can I stand on solid ground?
Rebuild my foundation?

So that when others,
Build on top of me...or journey alongside me...
They'll know...
They can count on me.

Because our common ground is *grounded* with Love.

Potato Duty
Sunny "Dos" Dosanjh

I'm not a peeler
But I have peeled

I was on potato duty
So I peeled

Did I peel enough
Maybe someone will tell me

Yes.

Mr. L
G. Craige Edgerton

My 12-year-old grandson has a fascination with war and guns. Me, not so much. I'm a combat Marine who served in Vietnam, and I am somewhat distraught with his fascination. But I can't help but be reminded that I followed a similar path when I was that age, as echoes of World War II were still present in the early 50s. I tromped through the scrub desert of South Texas with my friends among the Mesquite and Huisache brush, pretending to be Marines as we fashioned sticks into rifles. Oh, how we forget! But the stories I heard of WW II were of heroism, pride, and glory. No one ever told me the real truth of war. I was not going to let that be the situation with my grandson.

It happened almost by accident one evening just before he went to bed. My daughter encouraged me to read some of my most recent writings, and I shared a poem about throwing away my Marine Corps uniform just a few weeks after being discharged. He was listening and started asking a few questions.

"Bubba, what did you do in the war"? he boldly asked.

"I was an artillery officer. I was in charge of a 105-millimeter artillery battery, and we were stationed on a firebase."

"Yeah, but what did you actually do?"

"I ensured the 105s fired correctly when we got a target. I would receive radio information and relay it to the gunners, and they would prepare the rounds and fire them on my command."

I tried to explain to him in the most basic language without getting into too much detail. I gave a few simplified examples, but his rapt attention told me he wanted more.

"What kind of gun did you have"?

"I had a pistol and an M-16. Do you know what an M-16 is"?

"Oh yeah! I have a bunch of them in my Legos."

He is a Lego guru and has built battle scenes with his Legos, including the D-Day invasion of WWII, complete with landing crafts, tanks, soldiers, enemies, and emplacements. He has miniature weapons and can name them all correctly. He knew exactly what an M-16 was. His face lit up when he learned that I carried a real M-16. The next question piqued his curiosity.

"Did you ever shoot it?"

"Sure, in training, I practiced quite a lot."

"No, I mean for real. Did you shoot at anyone in the war?"

Here it was. This is what he really wanted to know. He had pretended with his Legos, but now he had a chance to ask someone, his grandad, what it was like to shoot a rifle at someone else. I didn't answer immediately. I looked up and pondered a bit before answering. I wanted to get this right.

"I was lucky that I never had to shoot at someone with my rifle. All of my shooting was with the 105's. I would have used it if the situation called for it, but it never did. Do you think you could shoot someone?"

He hesitated slightly before answering negatively, but he wasn't completely sure.

"I've fired my dad's AR, and it was fun."

"That is fine. Using weapons for target practice, hunting, or just for fun or protection is appropriate."

"I don't think I could ever shoot an animal, though."

His mom nodded at me, implying that he loves animals but cannot shoot one.

"Let me ask you another question. Is fire good or bad?"

A long pause ensued, with his finger to his chin looking upwards as his mind pondered the question. I could see his dilemma in answering this question.

"It depends on how it is used, I guess."

"Exactly. The same goes for weapons. They can be used for good or bad, depending on who has the weapon and what they are using it for. In war, both sides think they are doing good, yet they end up killing each other. And it is not a pleasant thing to do for either of them."

Mom ended the conversation at that time as she could see that I had made my point. I'm sure he will continue to play war with his Legos, but he at least now has a better sense of what war is about. Playing about war is one thing. Reality another.

Service

Jaime Johnson

O630 hours. Alarm goes off, waking me. I jump out of bed, excited for the day and its purpose. I almost rush it in the shower, as I'm so anxious that I can taste it.

Dressed and ready to get my gear. Bags of tools, cases of supplies, and a desire to put it all into motion.

0730 hours. On the road now, almost like I'm driving back to the FOB after a patrol. Gotta be careful to not mess this up. Overly aware and looking for hazards.

0800 hours. Arrive at my destination, relieved I made it and can get to work. Hump my gear and supplies to what will be my home for the next 6 hours.

Get things organized. A place for everything, and everything in place. Clear and clean, starting the process. Do it right, do it once.

0930 hours. Prepped and ready to work, I tear open the bags of fuel, dump the contents into the grill, soak it all, then light it up. I have brought life to my forge, allowing me to serve my brothers and their families, allowing me to have purpose ... even if its only for a short time.

CONTEXT: I BBQ at my veteran support group's pot-luck picnics, dating back to when I started cooking for our monthly benefits briefing we got from the Veteran Services Office. The reasons have changed, making sure everyone had something to eat during a long meeting at lunch time, but the underlining intent has not. This is my "process", my preparation to ensure that what I cook for them is the best I can bring forth for those who have suffered so much. For those who were treated so poorly by their government and their fellow Americans. Even though so many were drafted, they deserved so much more than the horrendous treatment that was literally spat and thrown at them by those they swore to protect.

Korean War Veterans Speech
Sunny "Dos" Dosanjh

You were never forgotten
Not by those who care
By those who understand

What do we understand?
One may ask?

Duty, Honor, Sacrifice
Is my reply.

In a Far Away Land
On the other side of our world
Our Young Men were sent – approximately 1.8 Million combat troops

Sent on a mission, To do what?
That still remains an open question – since technically the two sides are still at a stalemate
But back then it was to stem the spread of Communism across Asia

Our troops arrived in 1950 and they fought for three years
The battle lines across the 38th parallel were clear
North Koreans, Soviets, Chinese to the North
Americans and a host of countries as part of the United Nations, to the South

From one of the earliest battles, the Battle of OSAN
To the Battle of Inchon

To the Battle of Imjin River
Battle of Bloody Ridge
Battle of Chosin Reservoir
Battle of Heartbreak Ridge
To the many Battles for Seoul
Operation Commando
Operation Courageous
Operation Tomahawk
To the Battle of White Horse Hill

The cost to America was grave…over 38,000 died
Over 103,000 Wounded
Over 8000 POW's and MIA's
And 131 Medal of Honor Recipients

Our Leaders
From President Truman to President Eisenhower
Army General and Commander in Chief, Far East Command… Douglas MacArthur
Vice Admiral Arthur D. Struble, United States Navy
Major General Oliver P. Smith, United States Marine Corp
Rear Admiral James H. Doyle, United States Navy
Lieutenant General, George E. Stratemeyer, United States Air Force

Under their leadership, the allies pushed back the North Koreans across the 38th parallel
Eventually, an armistice signed in July 1953 brought the war to an end.
Over 5 million people died.

Some may have forgotten, some may have never known
For others, perhaps it's a footnote in a history book
But for those of us, who are part of the American Military Family
We remember.

"Freedom Is Not Free"
Here at home, located just southeast of the Lincoln Memorial, is the Korean War Memorial
19 sculptures of servicemen, on patrol in the fields
Their reflection, when reflected on a polished granite wall
Become 38
Representing the parallel that demarcates North and South Korea

Granite strips and scrubby juniper bushes suggest the rugged Korean terrain and vegetation
While windblown ponchos recall the harsh weather that tormented our troops and added to their misery.
This symbolic patrol brings together members of the Army, Navy, Air Force and Marines
And portrays servicemen from a variety of ethnic backgrounds.

The "Field of Service" culminates at the triangular dedication stone at the base of the flagpole

OUR NATION HONORS HER SONS AND DAUGHTERS
WHO ANSWERED THE CALL
TO DEFEND A COUNTRY
THEY NEVER KNEW
AND A PEOPLE THEY NEVER MET.

Ladies and Gentlemen,
If ever there was a reason to fight…
Then the model of South Korea…
In 70 short years

Has gone from rubble and disaster
To one of the global economic powerhouses

Once where there was darkness,
Now there is Light.

Moon Landing
Nick Butterfield

I finally found a path of broken
cement of what I thought
Vietnam was and is.

But as I walk along the cracks I
see new bricks being laid.

Hope is a ghost you no longer
have to believe in

seen in children's eyes as they land ,
as they remember the cracks from
where hope came.

Crumbled, Humbled and Welcomed Home

Sunny "Dos" Dosanjh

Crumbled is my life
Mind shattered into fragments of time
Body broken by father time

Crumbs swept away by winds with no name
Limbs weary from life's misery
Am I alive?

Thus the Squirrel threw an acorn at my head
The tree had many
And I laughed at my fortunate misfortune

Even the Squirrel felt my plight
And kindness was shown
Albeit, now with a bump on my head
So I laughed a laugh
that only the Gods understand

Laughter gave way to a smile
A smile gave way to gratitude
At least someone, a Squirrel of all things
Noticed my plight
And I was humbled
For now, mother nature saw her son

Mother, forgive me
Heal me, kill me or let me go

Now the spiders, wasps and bugs
had their turn also. So I surrendered

Closed my eyes, laid down under the tree
And started to fade into the mystic
Welcome Home, she said

There she stood, the divine feminine
Nourished my masculine warrior soul
Welcome Home, she said

Eyes opened
And a heart that was once broken
Now awakened to a new reality
Faith had welcomed me home

Redemption
G. Craige Edgerton

Can he live with the monster inside?
That subtle, or sometimes gargantuan,
Knowing of inadequacy,
Of moral injury, of a fraudulent persona,
Unable to relate to a world that can't understand?

The monster lives, a secret, not able to share.
The story's the same, the details different.
Hiding in the recesses of the warrior's mind,
Always present despite struggles to avoid.

For combat veterans
The monster is real.
Can be all-consuming.
Can rule or ruin lives.

The monster lives in his memories.
Pinned down, can't help.
"Mama! Mama!" the plaintive cry.
Brothers by birth; brothers by fire.
Why him and not me?

Bodies on the chopper floor.
Cleaning brains of a fallen comrade.
A gruesome initiation ritual for
The newly arrived warrior.

Cone hatted woman and child approach.
Finger nervously twitches on the M-60 machine gun.

One more step and I'll…
She stops and retreats into the twilight fog.

Viet Cong are invisible.
Jungle patrols flush them out.
Tripwire—exploding grenade!
Almost home intact. Purple Heart disdained.

Nightmares, booze, divorce, no secure job.
The monster is in control.
Regret, anger, moral injury, loneliness, ineptitude.
And yes, even suicide.

Yet in this maelstrom and turmoil
A barely perceived voice beckons, reminding him
Of his humanity, of his love, of his devotion
To the essence of his true self.

Those with the biggest, most vulnerable hearts
Get hurt the most.
If he didn't care, he wouldn't hurt.
His humanity is his redemption.

In battle, his comrades connect him to humanity,
The enemy, his separation from humanity.
In redemption, comrades also come to the rescue
By sharing, understanding, listening, forgiving.

Redemption isn't easy.
The memory can't be erased; the bell not un-rung.
Brothers in arms must come together once again,
Even if fifty years late.
But these arms embrace, not destroy.

These arms hold…understanding.
These arms encircle…his story, no judgment.
These arms listen…with a bear hug.
These arms are his forgiveness.

The warrior goes to battle with his brothers.
He must battle his monster with his brothers, too.
Redemption is not done alone.
It can only be done with his brother by his side.

Crows
M. Burgamy

Rising early I go to the garden
looking for refuge, coffee in hand hoping
to embrace the solace of morning birdsong,
some respite from the despair and desperation.

This day long ago, she left. Taxes were due.
And on this day the Tsarmaevs bloodied Boston.
News of Black boys here shot too close to home.
Today, everyday, haunting flashes from VietNam.

Coffee cooling in hand and heart-heavy,
The weight almost too much on this day,
I sit with my flowers, seeking sweet birdsong,
Only to be greeted by the cacophony of crows.

CHAPTER IV
Friends and Family

"I'd like to say that if you were a living human being fifty years ago in this country, you are a Vietnam veteran."
Doug Rawlings—former President, Veterans for Peace

Letter from a Veteran's Brother

Craige,

I want to clarify something important. After reading about what you have experienced and comparing it to how I was affected by Vietnam, I feel somewhat embarrassed to share my own story. What I experienced is but a small grain of sand compared to the life-altering experiences you have endured. I believe that what happened in Vietnam was a "one-of-a-kind" war. A war that we should all hope remains "one of a kind".

I also believe that the Vietnam debacle was unique in that it may have had more effect on Americans than any other confrontation America has undergone. That being said, I appreciate your interest in hearing my small story about how Vietnam affected me personally. I thought it would be easier to put it in writing. The story seems a little bogged down and complicated at times, but it all seemed important to me, so the details are included.

I grew up in South Texas and had two younger and two older brothers, along with one older sister. As common among larger families, each of the siblings grew into their particular role within the family structure. I always somehow perceived my siblings as being segmented into two different groups. One consisted of my older brother George, his sister Janie, and then the younger of that group, you.

The second tier of siblings would have been Randy, the youngest brother, Adrain, the next older brother; and then me. In my mind, the family segmentation and role-playing within the two tiers had implications in this story. Whether right or wrong, I believed that George, the oldest brother, took a more dominant role within the older tier of siblings. As the oldest of the younger I felt I took on the same leadership role as the three younger brothers.

So, being the oldest of the three younger brothers and being close but not quite old enough to be included in the older tier, I grew up perceiving myself as being in the middle, in sort of a neutral zone. During my formative years as an adolescent, I often went back and forth between leadership and subordinate roles. I saw myself as the leader in the younger tier and "wanna-be" in the older. George was significantly older than me in the older tier, so that relationship was somewhat separated. I felt more connected to Janie and you. There was often quarreling between Janie and me but in times of need, I always relied on her advice. I loved and respected her dearly but would never have allowed her to know that. In some ways, I was much like our dad.

The point of this story is that my experiences and feelings about Vietnam, in many ways, stem directly from my relationship with you. This whole story is "your fault," as young me often said to my parents. In reality, you were my "go-to" guy. I admired and looked up to you in every way. I admired the way you dressed, the way you acted, the way you thought, your athletic ability, your drive, and the way you interacted with your friends, both boys and girls. I wanted to be just like you. After all, how many dudes get to have a big bro like you?

So fast forward to the late 1960s and 70s. I headed to Lubbock and Texas Tech University to get an education. My real intent was to use Texas Tech as a launching pad to a professional baseball career. I was proud of my accomplishments at Tech, but because of an elbow injury, I was forced from the game of baseball. As a junior at Tech, I relinquished my scholarship and the game of baseball and began focusing on a post-college career and another way of life.

When you were about to graduate from college, another event was going on across the sea. Much like the rest of America, I was a little confused about Vietnam and could only read and listen to others giving their opinions on the war. This made it even more confusing. At or about that same time, a system called the lottery draft was introduced. This was a way of selecting military draftees for Vietnam. My lottery number was 32, so I knew I would be drafted upon graduation. Like my older brother, you, my choice was to attend OCS and go in as an officer or to join the ranks, serve my mandatory two years, and hopefully return from Nam to a normal life.

To understand this story, remember that, in my eyes, you were a hero. You were a bad-ass Marine who had chosen to go in as an officer and serve your country. I was unbelievably proud of you, and I often told my friends and bragged about my Marine big brother, who was currently in Vietnam. So, picture this scenario: My heroic brother is doing his job protecting our country in Vietnam, and now I am about to be drafted to do the same. I knew how courageous my brother was and realized that the only right thing to do would be for me to follow in his footsteps. The last thing in the world I would want would be to disappoint the guy I admired the most.

Also, remember that I perceived myself as an athlete and, in my own mind, knew I was in excellent physical condition and could hang with the best. I knew my elbow injury kept me from throwing a baseball, but also knew that such an injury would not keep me away from Vietnam. Understanding this is important to my mindset and eventual feeling of guilt.

At the time I was about to be drafted, there was horrible press going on about the happenings in Vietnam. In all reports there was absolutely nothing positive about our efforts there. Lives and limbs were lost for no reason. The horrible stories, pictures, and videos of mass murder and destruction of an entire country kept me awake at night. I was desperate to find a way to avoid being sent there.

The only way to avoid the draft was to find some physical defect prohibiting me from being drafted. Physical defect? Really? A college athlete in perfect physical condition is exactly who they were looking for. I knew this and it played on my psyche. I knew that if I failed the draft because of some physical issues, my big brother would forever be disappointed in me. I was totally aware that there was no physical defect in me. I knew I could never fool a Marine, especially my brother, who knew me well. So, how in hell's name could I intentionally avoid going to Vietnam when my blood brother, whom I admired so much, was there fighting for me and my country? How could I not do my part? And then how could I ever face the guy I most admired as a kid? How could I convince him that I had a physical defect? Forget it, no way. He knew of my athleticism and knew I was perfectly capable of serving in the war. The guilt set in even more.

To the earlier point about the two tiers of family structure, remember that I felt I was the leader and the supposed role model for the younger tier. So now, I was also dealing with the potential of setting a poor example for my two younger brothers if I decided not to defend my country. Right or wrong, I felt the responsibility rested directly on my shoulders. It was against my grain to set a bad example. By claiming disability, could I then also lose the respect of my two younger brothers? And then him? And then, ultimately, my entire family? I knew that my decision on how to handle my involvement in Vietnam would determine not only my own self-respect but also the respect I received from both tiers within my family for the rest of my life.

Shortly after I began to feel the self-inflicted guilt, the Vietnam War began to wind down. The military stopped taking draftees as the war was coming to an end. I sidestepped having to make the biggest decision of my life. I avoided having to step into a hell hole with no bottom. However, none of this altered the fact that my brother courageously served his country, and I did not. The guilt loomed on. Over time, I began to understand and realize that I was not a lesser person for not following in my brother's footsteps. I realized how fortunate I was. This realization made me even more thankful for my brother and the rest of the men and women who served in my place. In later life, I remained cognizant of and never forgot how thankful I was to those who served. I reached out to many wounded veterans and helped them in multiple ways.

Even though, in retrospect, everyone knew that Vietnam was a disaster, it did not diminish the fact that the men and women in our armed forces were willing to dedicate their lives to the country and people they loved.

So, Craige, what happened to me and how Vietnam affected me was minuscule compared to what happened to you. Mine was all internal; yours was much more. The excerpts you sent triggered some real feelings I have kept inside and have not shared until now. Not that my story is earth-shattering or exhibits some great revelation, but after reading about your PTSD, I wanted to share it with you. In my eyes, you were always a hero. Your being a Lieutenant in the United States Marine Corps during the Vietnam War made me stand tall. It made me proud to be an American and maybe more proud to be your brother.

Later on, I somehow knew that you had issues in Nam, but when I realized that you were embarrassed about your service and that you blamed yourself and America instead of corrupt and stupid politicians; it tore me up. Sorry, but I stand resolute that America, as a whole, did not do this. Politicians did. This way of thinking may be foreign to you and not how you perceive it. If so, I am sorry. But it's my way of allowing me to always take pride in who we are and where we live. Pride is important, and I choose to hang on to it as long as I can.

Unfortunately, the reason you were in Vietnam was not to do what you ended up having to do. I know, and most Americans now know, that you and others were there for what you thought would protect the men and women you cared most about—your family, your kids, and grandkids etc, etc. I feel sure that while in Vietnam, had you been able to accomplish what you hoped and thought you were sent to do, you would have an entirely different mindset and have a much different attitude when saying our Pledge of Allegiance. In my mind, you should not blame yourself for doing what you thought would be good, but rather the politicians that created the situation. They are the ones you should be mad at, not America, and damn sure not yourself.

The great thing about our country is that we have the option of removing those idiots from office and reelecting others that we think will do the right thing. In other places, this is not an option. Not to be trite, but as far as you knew, you were there to defend life, liberty, and the pursuit of happiness.

And that, brother, is noble and something you should always be proud of, no matter the outcome. I hope that someday, you can and will have pride in your military service. Not so much for what actually happened in Vietnam but for the fact that you were willing to stand up for what you believed. I truly hope you can transcend to this point, and I hope this story has a small roll in your ability to do that. But rest assured, whether you do or you don't, your younger brother will never stop being overly proud that you represented him and the rest of this country as a Lieutenant in the United States Marine Corps. Never.

Letters Home, 2nd Platoon ECHO

A nonymous—Tom Isenburg recalls this poem as a group effort of a handful of Marines in ECHO Company.

This poem was written by a group of Marines in December 1965 while in Vietnam.

We are surprised and angered by the anti-war demonstrations we read about from home. Please give the poem to our friends and relatives as a response to the demonstrators. We are beginning to feel that we are the only people who know why we have to win in Vietnam—to ensure former President Kennedy's legacy of stopping the spread of Communism.

WHO IS HE?

YOU SIT AT HOME AND WATCH TV.
YOU'RE SIPPING REFRESHING COLD ICED TEA.
THE NEWS COMES ON AND THEN YOU HEAR,
THE ALL-STAR GAME IS DRAWING NEAR.

THEN YOU SEE A FAR-OFF LAND
WHERE MEN ARE DYING ON THE SAND.
A FROWN APPEARS ACROSS YOUR FACE,
YOU'RE TIRED OF HEARING ABOUT THAT PLACE.
WHO CARES ABOUT VIETNAM ACROSS THE SEA?
IT'S FAR AWAY AND DOESN'T CONCERN ME.
YOU'D RATHER HEAR THE BEATLES PLAY,
THAN HEAR ABOUT THE WORLD TODAY.

BUT STOP AND THINK FOR A MOMENT OR TWO,

AND ASK YOURSELF, "DOES THIS CONCERN YOU?"
IT'S GREAT TO BE ALIVE AND FREE,
BUT WHAT ABOUT THE GUY ACROSS THE SEA?
HE'S GIVING UP HIS LIFE FOR ME,
SO THAT I CAN LIVE UNDER LIBERTY.
HE'S FAR AWAY FIGHTING A WAR,
INSTEAD OF FIGHTING AT MY FRONT DOOR.

THIS GUY WHO LIVES IN FILTH AND SLIME,
HOW CAN HE DO IT ALL THE TIME?
HE'S ABOUT MY AGE, SO WHY SHOULD HE CARE,
ABOUT A WAR SOMEONE ELSE SHOULD SHARE.

YOU CALL HIM VILE NAMES AND MAKE FUN OF HIS CAUSE,
YOU LUCKY GUY, YOU LAUGH AND SNEER,
BECAUSE YOU'VE NEVER REALLY KNOWN FEAR.
THIS YOUNG MAN FACES DEATH EACH DAY,
BUT HE ALWAYS HAS SOMETHING FUNNY TO SAY.

NO MAIL AGAIN? A TWINGE OF SORROW.
OH, WHAT THE HELL-THERE'S ALWAYS TOMORROW.
THE MORALE IS LOW, THE TENSION IS HIGH.
SOME EVEN BREAK DOWN AND CRY.
HE WANTS TO GO HOME AND SEE A LOVED ONE.
HE WORKS ALL DAY AND STANDS GUARD ALL NIGHT.
HE'S TIRED AND SICK, BUT HE CONTINUES TO FIGHT.

THE COLLEGE CROWD THINKS HE'S A FOOL,
BUT THAT'S WHAT MAKES HIM HARD AND CRUEL.
YOU DON'T APPRECIATE WHAT HE'LL DO,
LIKE GIVING UP HIS LIFE FOR YOU.
HE SACRIFICES MUCH YET ASKS NOTHING IN RETURN,
JUST SO YOU CAN STAY IN SCHOOL AND LEARN.

HE BELIEVES IN FREEDOM AND THE AMERICAN WAY
OF LIFE.
NO PARTIES OR DANCES FOR THIS YOUNG MAN,
UNTIL HE COMES BACK AGAIN.
THE DAYS ARE HOT, AND THE NIGHTS ARE TOO,
WHAT WONDERS A COLD CAN OF BEER CAN DO.
HE THINKS OF COLD BEER AND A THICK, JUICY STEAK,
WHEN SOMEONE SHOUTS "WE'VE GOT A HILL TO
TAKE."

SOME WILL BE HEROES BECAUSE THEY ARE BRAVE,
AND OTHERS WILL GET A WREATH ON THEIR GRAVE.
YOU'LL RECOGNIZE HIM AS HE WALKS BY.
THERE'S A SADDENED LOOK IN HIS EYE.
HE WALKS PROUD YET LOOKS SO MEAN,
HE'S CALLED THE "WORLDS GREATEST FIGHTING MA-
CHINE."
HE'S A UNITED STATES MARINE.

Abilene Airport
G. Craige Edgerton

It was small even for 1969.
Four gates, seldomly used,
A quaint snack bar. The Abilene Airport.
The last conversation with my Mom.

I packed my duffel bag.
She pretended to be busy.
Few words were spoken.
Her second son was off to war.

Torn between excited anticipation
And the dread of not ever coming home,
I assured her I'd be okay,
Trying to assure myself of the same.

I returned to that same airport,
The same quaint snack bar
Abilene, Texas, nine months later
After serving in Vietnam.
A First Lieutenant in the Marine Corps.

This time, she was not there to greet me.
She was at Scott and White Hospital
In Temple, Texas. Stage 4 cancer.
Less than 24 hours to live.

I saw her one last time,
Adorned in my dress blues,
She, barely conscious.

Her faint smile the last communication.

If only I had known.
If only she had known.
That the conversation
At Abilene Airport
Would be our last.

Helicopter OH-6A 67-16162
Carol Steele

Danny Owens was stationed on a ship
on a river in Dong Tam, South Vietnam.
Awakened in the middle of the night, he rolled out,
pulled on his uniform and took the stairs
two at a time to the flight deck.
Our soldiers on shore were under fire.
He climbed in the cockpit, started the aircraft,
was given the thumbs up and lifted off.

His mom sat in the top row of the bleachers
at school baseball games, screaming cuss words at him.
He was 6'2" with blue eyes and brown hair,
strong and kind to me. When my boyfriend and I broke up,
Danny and I spent hours in his '57 white Chevy
driving the high Sierra mountain roads.
I don't remember what we said
as much as how comfortable I felt next to him.

When I moved away from Mt. Shasta
Danny came to visit. We stayed up that night
in his motel room leaning against the headboard, talking.
He said he loved me; was signed up for the service
but wouldn't go if I married him.
In the morning, we stood in the parking lot, soft yellow light
surrounding him and hugged goodbye.
We talked on the phone a couple of times
and then I didn't hear from him.

The report says he lifted off, hovered

and when he should have gained airspeed,
lost altitude. The skids skimmed the water.
the helicopter tipped forward and crashed
sinking rapidly. They sent two planes
searching all night but couldn't find him
or his chopper.

It was years before I heard how he died.
My first thought was I wish I had made love with him.
At least he would have had that.
Now, alone a long time and still remembering,
I wish we had made love.
At least I would have that.

Biographies

Nick Butterfield

Nick AKA Nektarios Butterfield served in the USNR as a Hospital Corpsman HM1 from 1983 to 1993. Active during Operation Desert Storm and Desert Shield in 1990-1991 "Grief is the source of many of my writings. PTSD, I saw in my dad who was a Pearl Harbor Survivor and many of my current writing collaborators. They are not just veterans of war but of life."

Nick was one of the few who gathered in Willow Glen Bookstore in the mid-90s. The Willow Glen Poetry Project went on to publish 3 anthologies in which Nektarios participated in. He has contributed to 3 Caesura editions in the past and contributed to Veterans of Life Write book that came out in 2020.

He co-facilitates Veterans of Life Zoom meetings the first Friday of every month which is sponsored by the Psychology Dept. at SJSU and Martin Luther King Library and Poetry San Jose. The group has participated in seven Poetry San Jose Festivals and has been meeting regularly since 2015. A group that started with Amy Meier's recognition of a need for Veterans to write and heal.

R. Marshall Burgamy

Burgamy served in the U.S. Marine Corps from 1967 to 1971 after dropping out of college in his sophomore year. After completion of Boot Camp at MCRD San Diego, and Infantry Training at Camp Pendleton, CA, he attended Basic Disbursing School in Camp Lejune, N.C. and later the NCO Leadership Academy at Quantico, VA, graduating second in each of his classes. He arrived in VietNam May1969, first posted at Quang Tri Combat Base, then at Dong Ha Combat Base in I Corps with the 3rd Battalion of the 3rd Marine Division some 6 miles from the DMZ. In 1970 he was posted to Okinawa, from which he served on float with the 29th Marines and the Air Wing aboard the LPH (Landing Platform Helicopter) New Orleans and then the Tripoli. Both LPHs returned to VietNam as part of their combat missions.

He served in the Marine Corps with his cousin, James Dale Palmer, who was severely wounded in fierce combat and never fully recovered before dying much too young.

After his service Burgamy returned to college, then graduate school, and law school before joining the Peace Corps where he served for two and a half years in Costa Rica. He was honored to be named a Harvard Teaching Fellow in 1981. He has taught university in Kuwait, Malaysia, and Costa Rica. Burgamy ended his career in education as a principal and a director of public schools with the Sequoia Union High School District in California. He is the proud father of Corinne Reneé, and overjoyed with his grandchildren, Andres Gael and Camila Reneé. He is fortunate to have found Patti Crisafi, the love of his life in his twilight years.

Burgamy attempts to live a life of gratitude and remembrance of all those VietNam veterans not as fortunate. He appreciates the VA, his counselor Daniel Boitano, and his fellow Vets in the San Jose PTSD group for their support and healing. He gives thanks to Craige Edgerton for his vision, drive and leadership through the creative process to bring our stories to fruition and publication.

Sunny Dosanjh

The moon entered into Waning Gibbous with an illumination of 82% on the day I was born at 8am, October 1st, 1968 in London, England. There were no seismic shifts in society, no trumpets heralding a new life but I can imagine the joy of my parents. That's enough for me.

Raised in England and in Turlock, California, I joined the United States Air Force at 17 years of age. I served honorably and used the GI Bill at San Jose State University for a Bachelor's in Management Information Systems, earned in 1994. The next 30 years were in High Tech all while marrying, divorcing and fathering three offspring.

My goal at age six was to understand love. Now, at age 56, I know and understand love. My contributions to this book chronicle my journey from my Military years to present day. I now volunteer as an American Legion Chaplain, Captain of the Honor Guard and Service Officer. On October 1st, 2024, the moon was a Waning Crescent with an illumination of 15%. My light still shines and I hope these stories inspire you!

G. Craige Edgerton

Craige started his writing practice at age 75, as suggested by his Vet Center counselor to help him deal with his negative issues regarding his time in Vietnam as a combat Marine. He fought it for many months and finally decided to try it just once. It turned out to be one of the best decisions of his life and he hasn't stopped.

In college, he admired those who could write creatively and tell compelling stories. But being from rural South Texas, he lacked confidence. And who would want to hear his story of a very ordinary life anyway?

The counseling sessions at the Vet Center that dealt with his, and many others, PTSD made him realize that being in combat was not an ordinary experience. Very few individuals have such experiences. He realized that the stories of the mostly Vietnam veterans were unique, not in actual combat stories, but in how they had recovered fifty-plus years later.

For reasons that are still unclear, he decided to write some of those stories and enroll others willing to tell their stories too. This book is the result of that decision.

Jaime Lee Johnson

Born in San Jose, California, Jaime Lee Johnson was raised by his aunt after an adoption at a very early age. She married shortly after and he lived a relatively normal childhood. Friends, did well in school, and loved sports. Especially ice hockey.

Jaime knew he wanted to serve, given how every generation in his family had in one way or another, but also knew it was a commitment. He served 7 years in the US Army as an infantryman and in a military intelligence unit. Including a deployment to Baghdad in 2005.

After discharging, he experienced trouble like most vets with PTSD and had to find help for it. A friend recommended he go to the Vet Center in San Jose and everything changed. He got the help he needed and found a new home of sorts with the support groups he attends to this day.

Jaime knew that the lessons he learned through the group could help others, which is why he became part of the project for this book. He wanted to pass on his experiences with PTSD and how he found ways to deal with the side effects of war, both physically and mentally. He hopes that with this book, he can help at least one veteran reconnect with their family or their friends. Or to show them the way on getting help for problems they feel no one else can understand.

Doug Nelson

Doug Nelson grew up in Richmond, Virginia.

Bored with college, he enlisted in the army and spent a year in Vietnam listening to Viet Cong communications/Morse code and surviving a mortar attack.

He finished college after spending 2 years in Japan.

After a career in the Federal Government (Army Civil Service),

Doug has enjoyed traveling, writing poetry, and spending time with his family.

Bill Noyes

Born in San Francisco in September 1947, Bill was raised in Honolulu, Hawaii, and then again in San Francisco. He graduated in 1965 from A. Hill High in San Jose and then attended San Jose State College. In 1967, Bill was drafted into the Vietnam War, B 2/22, earning a Silver Star and a Combat Infantry Badge north of Saigon. He finally earned his BA degree from SJ State U. in Philosophy in 1978.

Bill married in 1976 and raised two daughters, Regina and Tiana (Xollie), at their Campbell home. He retired from welding after 30 years. During this time, he worked on various home additions, sculpted statues, and persisted with writing projects and books. War experiences have taken much of his attention throughout his life and, accordingly, resulted in many valuable lessons learned.

ABOOKS

ALIVE Book Publishing and ALIVE Publishing Group
are imprints of Advanced Publishing LLC,
3200 A Danville Blvd., Suite 204, Alamo, California 94507

Telephone: 925.837.7303
alivebookpublishing.com